Miami

A Backward Glance

Miami

A Backward Glance

Muriel V. Murrell

Pineapple Press, Inc.
Sarasota, Florida

To Jack with love

Inquiries should be addressed to:

Pineapple Press, Inc.
P.O. Box 3889
Sarasota, Florida 34230

www.pineapplepress.com

Library of Congress Cataloging-in-Publication Data

Murrell, Muriel V.
    Miami, a backward glance / Muriel V. Murrell
        p.   cm.
    Includes index.
        ISBN 1-56164-286-X (alk. paper)
    1. Miami (Fla.)—History—20th century. 2. Miami (Fla.)—History—20th century—Pictorial works. 3. Miami (Fla.)—Description and travel. I. Title.
        F319.M6 M86 2003
        975.9'38106—dc21
                                                    2003006308

First Edition
10 9 8 7 6 5 4 3 2 1

Design by Shé Heaton
Printed in the United States of America

Acknowledgments

*I*t was with the generous help and support of friends and well wishers that this book was completed. Such encouragement and positive urgings to continue—in the form of research, stories recalled and freely offered, technical expertise, and photographs—made the initial idea a reality between two covers, and I want to acknowledge the important part everyone played.

My gratitude and thanks go to Elizabeth Lewis Bedall, whose family lived at Vizcaya for a period of time; to Jean Rowntree Davis for anecdotes from the Davis property in the Grove; to Julia Allen Field, who even provided a notebook for jotting down midnight inspirations; to Rev. Thomas Niblock of Plymouth Church, who shared Vizcaya legends; to Mac Russell, who offered early photos of the area and the use of his scanning equipment; and to Betty Kaynor for her delightful story and alligator birthday cake picture. Maddy Geoghan passed along a wealth of Miss Harris' material that had been kept by Jean Perdue. Lucille Wilkenson was the first to see an early draft and find it readable. Even those who will be surprised to find themselves described in these pages must be acknowledged. Thanks to all.

Blue ribbons to my daughters, Sylvie and Victoria, who are responsible for the core of this work with regard to research and technical know-how, without which nothing gets done in today's world. Sylvie, especially, was diligent in pursuing loose ends. I commend both of them for being so patient with an author who kept asking, "Is it done yet?"

Lastly, bouquets for my editors, June Cussen and Kris Rowland, who guided this work from the desktop to the marketplace with a professionalism and good humor that made compliance a pleasure.

If I have missed an acknowledgment, forgive me. I will always remember the many who have buoyed me in this venture for their kind words and good advice.

Contents

1

On Looking Back

Once the fishing grounds of the Tequesta and Calusa Indians, Miami is now the playground of the rich and famous, as well as those who just love the sun. Miami evolved from the southernmost, scrub pine–littered mainland of the United States to a center of sophisticated living through the determined efforts of early settlers, who ignored the wilderness and swamps, mosquitoes and hurricanes, in order to plant their homesteads and cultivate this spot of great natural beauty. They scraped out roads, built homes, grew what would grow, and persisted in the face of boom times, economic depression, and war to establish Miami's position today as a worldwide mecca. In between these two extremes lie the vanishing traces of people who pioneered a frontier and made it home, each bringing his or her own vision and reasons for coming. Along the way, anecdotes emerged that recall a few of those early residents and the spaces in which they lived.

Some original houses from the early decades are still here in this place known far and wide as the Magic City. Their bones may be hidden from the view of newer neighbors or stripped of the protective trees and shrubbery among which they were first placed, so you will have to imagine how they blended into the new tropical city of which they were then a part. Some may have been transformed by additions or renovations, making them hard to recognize. Still others can be found, sadly, only in faded brown photographs or in the personal recollections of pioneers. These last structures were replaced, inevitably, by the relentless needs of Miami's growing and dynamic commercial world as it sped past the millennium. In a strange way, you could almost say that their occupants followed the same pattern over the years: some stayed put, some took on new looks, and some left, never to return, supplanted by business professionals now filling the lofty towers of global corporations.

The houses I remember most clearly are not just buildings from the past but echo chambers that vividly evoke for me the interesting people who once lived in them. Their contributions to today's Miami can be glimpsed through the small footnotes or trivia about them, tales still warm and funny and revealing of early Miamians, who coped with being pioneers in a subtropical world subject to alligators, hurricanes, eternal summer, and long distances from most big cities. These people and their stories should not be forgotten when we revisit their past haunts. They are not all celebrities nor historically important, but they are a significant part of the whole, and they left lasting impressions, helping to shape the present community. They were here.

We are who we are today, as a community, because of who they were.

2

Starting from Scratch

The Late Twenties

As a native Miamian, I remember early Miami in the late 1920s as a town with lots of vacant lots to play in; coconut palms in thick plantings; tough, indestructible palmettos everywhere; sandspurs all along the sand dunes covering the sweeping emptiness of the beachfronts that seemed to stretch toward forever; and sidewalks and lampposts often out in the middle of nowhere, signs of some developer's scheme too ambitious for its time.

Houses in the 1920s were usually built in the bungalow style. You can still see their look-alikes today in Little Havana, then known as Riverside Heights and Grove Park. Some still serve as residences with a Latin flavor, their ruling center now called Calle Ocho, once simply SW 8th Street. Others were converted to funeral homes and florist shops when the area was no longer residential.

It wasn't until George Merrick's Coral Gables (once a grapefruit grove with carriage tracks lying a good day's trek from downtown Miami) popularized the Spanish style and North Bay Road on Miami Beach upgraded to the grander

. . . and coconut palms everywhere along the beachfront.

Mediterranean and Italian villas that variety began to surface. Not all of the architectural ideas put forth were in harmony with their setting, however, or the subtropical climate or even the comfort of those who lived in them.

If you drive through the Gables today, you can see some of the novelty architecture in the villages created by George Merrick's plan, in the Chinese, French, Dutch, and Italian enclaves, which were erected in charming little isolated groups, the empty lots and wandering streets around them anticipating future growth. These, however, were a developer's ideal (a forerunner, perhaps, of Disneyworld?) and the outgrowth of a philosophy that holds there should be a certain congeniality in neighborhoods. What a far cry from the individual expressions of character often found in the dwellings of Miami and Coconut Grove!

Northern architects, admired in their own backyards,

were brought here by many wealthy winter residents in the town's early years. They created imposing edifices reflecting the status of their owners, construction that would look at home in Chicago or Connecticut but often appeared too dark, too heavy, too enclosed for Miami's gentler climate. In fact, it has taken the advent of air conditioning to make those still left really habitable.

Early photographs of the area west of the shoreline show vast, sandy expanses of land with scraggy pines, wild native brush, and a house here and there. Nothing like the shoulder-to-shoulder look of today's city. As for the beautiful green landscaping that seems so natural today? That was hard won in those days.

A lawn as we now know it required much work, lots of money, and never-ending patience. This was because the indigenous soil was a sort of sandy, gray dirt. Water stood on it like little globules of mercury, refusing to leave the surface, where "doodlebugs" and anthills abounded. Sometimes, in desperation, that soil was dug out to a depth of three feet, mixed with muck and marl from the Everglades, sifted through giant screen boxes by a man with a hoe, then replaced and planted with sprigs of St. Augustine grass. If a green sward grew, chinch bugs often took care of it with ugly, brown, spreading patches (no chemical sprays available then) and armyworms and the holes left by crabs were an ongoing nuisance. The solution settled on by my best friend's father was to save his cigar butts and stuff them down the holes to poison the crabs. (He swore it worked.)

Pioneers, first in line, were choosy about home sites. They preferred high ground. It caught the breeze if there was any, minimized the chance of snakes and scorpions finding their way into or under the house, and, with luck, provided a firm, coral rock base for the foundation as well as a porous drain for rainwater.

Early residents tended to be wary of waterfront property. Though it had its charms, silver blackened quicker, wool rugs stayed damp, oil paintings had to be wiped clean of mold, and any leather, including shoes in the closet, grew green fungus. It was a bad place to be in a hurricane too. With no sophisticated warning systems as we have today, the homeowner was often caught with his awnings down, ripped to shreds. (I can still recall the frustration in the voice of one radio announcer who was unaware his microphone was still open after a hurricane bulletin. "Well, if it isn't *there,* where the hell *is* it?" he demanded.)

Houses that didn't have porches needed awnings to keep out the relentless sunshine. My mother told me that when she came here as a young bride, many of the roads were of crushed coral rock—perfect for bouncing blinding reflections of the summer sun off their packed white surfaces, and in constant need of dampening to control the powdery dust that rose from the surface. In addition to relieving the glare, awnings also brought relief from a tedious chore. Without them, all the windows had to be closed when leaving the house, for quick-passing, tropical showers invariably rained in, leaving puddles on the windowsills and floor. Even more

Typical 1920s' bungalow with awnings.

undesirable, closing all the windows (an exhausting task with wooden windows that were often balky in the humidity) meant returning to a stuffy house that needed time to cool down and regain a bearable temperature. A few newcomers realized the potential for using natural foliage, the breeze-catching advantages of wide verandas and high ceilings, and the cooler atmosphere that could be created by all-white buildings, thus dictating the evolving look of the city.

Among Miami's earliest builders were the Brickells. The Mary Brickell homestead took in most of the land along Biscayne Bay south of the Miami River as far as the James Deering property, present-day site of Vizcaya. The pioneer family constructed several homes, all similar, all near Brickell Avenue and SE 8th Street, an area that was then heavily studded with old live oak trees. One of these large white houses was the first Brickell home, which sat at the mouth of the Miami River on the south side as it empties into the bay. (The Sheraton Hotel occupied that spot later). Today, all that is left of the original homestead that once encompassed that choice and verdant location is the parcel known as Brickell Park, with its graceful shade trees and Brickell family mausoleum. Maude Brickell, daughter of William and Mary Brickell, was said to have buried some of her beloved cats nearby.

At the turn of the twentieth century, this riverfront location was convenient for the Seminoles, who came down the Miami River wearing their colorful dress (said to be their interpretation of Scottish plaid) on flat-bottom boats and cypress dugouts to trade with the Brickells. Early arrivals noted in their journals that the fresh water of the Miami River, tumbling down from rapids, was so clear you could see the pale sand at the bottom of the riverbed. Fish and turtle were so plentiful in those days that turtle appeared on the menu in many boarding houses guised as "lamb," "beef," or "pork." Alligators and snakes (cottonmouths, rattlers, and deadly corals) were often seen and were to be avoided at all costs, and small creatures such as raccoons, bobcats, and possum lived along the river's banks. For all its great plans for the future, Miami was, after all, still very much a frontier, just a step from the Everglades. Fort Dallas was almost downtown. In fact, a friend who lived in one of the first homes on Alhambra Circle said that, as a child, he could hear the alligators in the nearby Gables Waterway canal by the Biltmore golf course grunting and calling at night a block from his house.

These Brickell houses were much alike in design: two- or three-story, modified Greek Revival style with tall Doric or Corinthian columns. They were formed of large blocks of oolite limestone, often called "Miami Rock," which had been chiseled out of the ground, then cut and axe-hewn by hand to a beveled appearance, and finally whitewashed, the whole often capped with a shingle or tin roof in the Key West style.

Unfortunately, none of those chalk-hued mansions in their groves of native hardwood, predominantly oak and pine, and graced by low, running coral rock walls, still stands. Even the very special skill required to fashion the rock walls themselves—the painstaking fitting together of natural rock shapes without cement—was a native craft brought to the area by Bahamian fishermen and almost forgotten today. It took local residents far too long to recognize the value of that part of the city's heritage. In the course of time, those sites became far more valuable as footpads for the banks and office buildings now in their stead. Alas, by then Brickell Avenue had changed forever. As appraisers say, "Highest and best use." Debatable.

As for Claughton Island (now known as Brickell Key) and its bridge at the end of SE 8th Street, that was not even a gleam in Biscayne Bay's eye. It was simply an infant spoil bank formed from the dredging of Government Cut. Peppered with young pines from the seeds sown by birds fly- ing overhead, the spoil bank grew and grew, thanks to the tides and natural erosion. Today, of course, high-rises there are so closely built, little of the island itself can even be seen. Just enough room to drive up and valet park.

As Miami spread along its shores, islands caught the

fancy of early developers. Waterfront for everyone, they proposed. Why not? And so the noise of barges pumping fill ran night and day, surveyors' stakes dotted the surface of the bay on either side of the causeways, and sober gray pelicans found the posts handy perches when tired of fishing—one to a customer. But, as the natives knew, islands composed of man-made fill pumped from the bay bottom were too low to be safe from tidal surges and hot to live on. In addition, osmosis, evident in veins of discoloration (not unlike Roquefort cheese), often caused damp to seep up into the walls of the houses until builders finally learned to put a metal barrier below the subflooring. Dig four feet down for a house foundation on these islands even today and there is yellow, brackish water. Houses built on low land still hide one-third of their cost in the underground pilings that support them, a necessary construction expense responsible for their higher prices. Buyers of early construction also learned to their dismay that concrete should not be made with salt water in the mix (a common mistake during the boom years). It corroded and twisted the steel supports of a house, producing a condition that seemed to melt the structure, as

Bird's-Eye View, Venetian and County Causeways, Miami Beach, Florida

The islands kept appearing.

palm plantation, was not even on the drawing board. The island could be reached only by boat.

The most admired portion of the Mary Brickell homestead was the land closest to the bay, where a long ridge of coral rock ran southward. It went through Coconut Grove and continued down to Snapper Creek canal, sloping off from there. This ridge formed a bluff of varying elevations, from near sea level to seventeen feet above. Its infrastructure offered firm anchorage for the beautiful mansions that were eventually built on it, together with superb views of the bay.

The rich strip of land that comprised the original Mary Brickell homestead also covered an area just west of the ridge that included the lush growth of many dense hammocks of live oak trees. These wonderful specimens are choosy about their location, are not easily transplanted, and create a soil that is perfect for ferns and tropical shade plants. Along the Miami River and southward, they graced the bayfront and could be found in small patches that stretched as far south as the Coral Gables Waterway. Their look is preserved in and formed the basis of Simpson Park at 15th Road and South Miami Avenue. In their cool, deep shade could be found all manner of native animals and insects; in their rough branches (brittle in hurricanes), orchids and other epiphytes bloomed all year round. The Florida panther, possum, and raccoon hunted at night within the trees' boundaries; during the day, they were home to tropical birds of all feathers. Tree snail colonies, with individual shell patterns for different families, hid in their deep recesses. But the thick, soft, leaf compost that accumulated year after year beneath them, giving off that distinctive odor of mold and damp, could be treacherous underfoot. It often disguised jagged sinkholes, pits created by flowing underground streams (plentiful below the porous rock) that suddenly changed direction so that the unsupported crust of rock crumbled, causing the surface above to cave in. A word to the unwary was in order: it was a place that was best left to nature's denizens.

Given the options their land afforded, William Brickell and his wife, Mary, chose to build the family home on the south bank of the Miami River as the twentieth century came into view. There, where the fresh water of the river meets Biscayne Bay, they set up a trading post. Other family members eventually built homes nearby, forming a sort of compound around SE 8th Street. Their neighbors seldom saw them, and they were considered odd and reclusive. Some wondered if William Brickell might be a fugitive. Trading with the Seminoles and acquiring property seemed to be their chief activities.

Eventually the original house was left in the care of Maude Brickell, spinster daughter of William and Mary, as succeeding generations of Brickells found other residences. Living alone with her numerous cats, she remained there until her death in 1960. She was considered by many to be eccentric in her dress and manner and rather formidable, and she may well have been. But no one could dispute her devotion to the many pets that roamed her property.

Mac Flowers, an Alabaman who came here as a young attorney at the turn of the 1920s, told me this story about the house and Maude Brickell. Like a number of other young bachelors who worked in the downtown offices, he once rented a room there. He remembered that in those days Maude Brickell had an old dog she was particularly fond of. Chester was a faithful hound of uncertain ancestry that followed her everywhere and could usually be found lying stretched on the wide porch taking the sun or sleeping under one of the big oak trees that filled the property.

Very late one evening, Mac recalled, after everyone had retired and the house was dark, Chester returned from a night's hunting and, finding the door barred, demanded to be let in. The sudden commotion as he threw himself against the screen, barking and whining, eventually roused one of the downstairs boarders. The groggy tenant, having been out partying most of the night, had just fallen into a deep state of unconsciousness and, unsure about the source of the noise, assumed burglars were trying to break down the door or a marauding bobcat was outside. Half awake, he managed to find his pistol, and in this somnolent state he aimed at the door and fired a single warning shot into the darkness.

A numbing silence followed. The other tenants, rudely awakened and alarmed by the noise, stumbled toward the scene of the uproar, which had not yet awakened their landlady. Cautious investigation revealed a terrible mistake had been made—Maude Brickell's favorite dog had been accidentally and irrevocably dispatched to that big hunting ground in the sky. Disbelief turned to dismay and, finally, to the dawning realization of the consequences this unfortunate happening would bring. It certainly took away all thoughts of going back to bed.

Not surprisingly, no one wanted to be the one to explain the sudden demise of Miss Brickell's longtime pet to her, yet there was a body to be dealt with. After all suggestions had been considered, it was finally agreed there was only one thing to be done. And to this end, a silent little group of conspirators, moving furtively into the heavy brush that edged the property and aided by the dark of the moon, hastily buried the unlucky animal.

Many times in the following days, Maude Brickell searched and called, wondering where her old dog could have gone. No one had the courage to tell her the awful truth. In time, as the days passed and the missing Chester failed to appear, she shook her head and concluded he must have wandered away or met an unfriendly alligator, thoughts that were readily encouraged by her guilt-stricken boarders.

It has come to light since then that there are lots of bones buried on that land, now called Brickell Park. The Brickells themselves built a family mausoleum under the spreading live oak trees. Even today, as ground is excavated for the new condominiums, banks, and offices marching south, there are fresh indications that the earliest Indians might have used the spot as a burial mound. But not all of the bones that rest there are Brickell or Indian, as revealed by Mac's story. Some remains sequestered in that park belong to Maude Brickell's old dog, Chester, and, rumor has it, even a cat or two found it a place to stay.

But Brickell Avenue, mindful of its potential, continued to evolve and, from its homely beginnings, has become the address of choice for thousands.

4

*W*ill the Last Parrot Please Turn Off the Lights?

Miss Harris' School

Miss Harris' Florida School for Girls occupied one of the Brickell-type houses at 1051 Brickell Avenue. A beautiful property that was two hundred feet wide and stretched more than one thousand feet east to Biscayne Bay, it was purchased in 1922. Today the site is occupied by a huge complex of offices, the 1101 Building.

The school was for girls from kindergarten through twelfth grade and was founded in 1914 by Julia Fillmore Harris, a Minnesota spinster with a degree in psychology, piercing blue eyes that could see right through you, and a tendency to hum when she was concentrating. The school's purpose was to demonstrate her firm belief in the benefits of a natural environment on one's health and in the idea of open-air classrooms. A healthy mind in a healthy body was the main goal, and the overriding concept was to encourage individual achievement while developing character along the way. The student body could boast an "aviatrix" who flew her own plane, a national skeet-shooting champion, and a qualifier for the U.S. Olympic swim team. In later years, a few boys whose sisters were enrolled were admitted, some for private tutoring. Their diplomas read, "Florida Scientific Preparatory School." (A student who later went to Princeton said his recurring nightmare was that his friends would discover he had spent the winter months of five school years at a school for girls.)

There were never more than 250 students enrolled, far fewer than that during the Depression. The classrooms were simple, one-story pavilions consisting of two walls made of blackboards and one wall of screening. The fourth side of each pavilion was open to the elements, thus providing as much fresh air as you could get. A single light bulb hanging from an electric cord in the center of each room was the sole light on infrequent rainy days. Most of the time these spartan accommodations sufficed. But on very cold days, not unknown in this clime (weather brought by visitors from the North, we said), the school *in toto* moved to the Main

Miss Harris' Lower School. Even dolls attended in the 1920s.

House, where we sat on rugs and cushions strewn on the polished hardwood floors in front of roaring open fires. If it got *too* cold, say, fifty degrees, everyone was sent home.

The Main House was the most substantial building of the school and sat in the center of the grounds at the end of a long drive lined with old oak trees and ending in a wide circle. Built in the usual Brickell fashion of whitewashed Miami rock, it featured a three-story porte-cochere surmounted by a sleeping porch, which had wide, green-painted verandas facing east and south. Tall columns with Corinthian capitals held the upper stories in place, and the sprawl of low, brown classroom pavilions around it made it seem a gracious white

The Main House: a gracious white beacon in its setting of feathery green palms.

beacon among feathery green palms and riotous pink and red bougainvillea, the blue of Biscayne Bay its backdrop.

The first floor held the music room, which contained two grand pianos for lessons and recitals; the office, for bookkeeping and phone messages; the faculty dining room and kitchen, from whence emanated the aroma of ginger-bread cake on Tuesdays; and a library with a tall, carved-mantel fireplace. A long dogtrot of polished, wide-board, dark hardwood divided the ground floor. This passageway was scattered with small Oriental rugs and runners, straight-back carved Italianate chairs spaced against the walls, and, above those, a large plaster cast of Michelangelo's *Madonna and Child*. Here the student body gathered for school-made movies and piano recitals. Years later, when the building was final-ly razed by a developer, some of this flooring found its way to the Jamaica Inn Restaurant on Key Biscayne (built by one of the Mathesons), and a lucky local couple acquired the original French doors in the music room for their Coral Gables home.

On the second floor of the Main House were bedrooms for the youngest boarding students. Miss Harris' rooms were on the third floor, where she lived with her mother, Mrs. Greeley, a frail lady in her nineties who never appeared without a black velvet ribbon and cameo brooch at her throat. Miss Harris' private door was always closed and had a small basket attached. This served as a receptacle for notes, mail, and house keys borrowed by faculty members who lived on campus during a rare evening out to accept dinner invitations, attend recitals, etc. The house being locked for the night, they were expected to drop the keys in this bas-ket when they returned. New young teachers who some-times overstayed their curfews were confident this was so Miss Harris could hear the clink of the keys and note the hour of their return. One young woman, having forgotten to take the key on her night out, had to be helped through an unlocked kitchen window by her hosts of the evening. She thought forced entry was the better part of valor. Luckily, Miss Harris was not given to watching kitchen windows, though not much else escaped her attention.

One fine spring day, a terrible odor was noticed coming from the boarding students' rooms on the second floor. It was the talk of the school. An exterminator was called to search for a possible dead rat or crab in the walls, a not uncommon problem in those days. Much fruitless dislocation of students and upturning of their belongings produced no answer to the steadily fuming mystery, raising the possibility that a contractor might have to be called to demolish part of the wall, an expensive undertaking. Finally, one of the maids discovered that a student who had not used all of his shrimp bait fishing off the dock had simply discarded it in

Looking east from the Main House, with aboveground pool and tennis court in the background.

The bay was important to us.

the flower box outside his window. As in a science experiment, sun and nature had produced the predictable pungent aroma, which took a long week to dispel.

The school grounds also contained a concrete tennis court. To inaugurate the opening of the court, U.S. tennis champion Don Budge, his older brother and coach, Lloyd, and Dr. William McKibben, Miami's first pediatrician, showed off their strokes. Budge, still in his early twenties, was one of only five tennis greats to win all Grand Slams in his career. In fact, the term *Grand Slam* was coined to describe his impressive record. A small, aboveground swimming pool was also located on the grounds. Surrounded by palms, it was where boarders were allowed to skinny-dip on weekend nights.

The bay was important. With no sea wall to impede us, we were free to explore the shoreline. Low tide gave us mossy stepping stones that reached a few feet out into the shallow green water. We searched for bleeding-tooth snails and limpets at recess; caught fiddler crabs to keep in brown Saltine cans with bay mud in the bottom; studied for tests while feeling the salt breeze from the water; and listened to the wind make sighing sounds as it passed through the Australian pines we now know as casuarinas. To the horizon stretched the liquid aquamarine and pale blue of the ocean as it flowed toward the deeper Gulf Stream, where we could see specks of far-off sails moving slowly. Our own sailboat, named *Viking*, was skippered by Mr. White, the athletic director (his wife was Chief Mate) for cruising the bay on Saturday outings. And everywhere in those days were clusters of graceful palms full of coconuts.

Attending school on the bay meant that uncommon events would sometimes mark our days. On one occasion, we were marshaled down to the water to await a promised surprise. One of our classmates, Helen Rudd Owen, was the granddaughter of William Jennings Bryan (Bryan Memorial Church in Coconut Grove is named for him) and the daughter of Ruth Bryan Owen Rohde, then serving as Congresswoman from Florida. A few years later, in 1933, President Roosevelt appointed her United States Minister to Denmark, the highest diplomatic post ever given a woman until that time. Mrs. Owen, a friend of Miss Harris, had been invited to visit the campus that day. It was a sunny morning, no clouds visible, and as we stared out at the shimmering bay, a small seaplane appeared, circled, and touched down lightly on the rippled surface. Out stepped Mrs. Owen to loud applause. She was then rowed ashore—it was rather like the landing of Ponce de León—to address the school assembly. I don't remember what she said to us, but her arrival was unforgettable, especially astonishing to youngsters in an age when planes overhead were a rarity. In fact, in those days, we often ran outside whenever we heard droning motors, hoping to catch a glimpse of some small craft approaching.

What did fly overhead from time to time, like a sudden storm, were the hundreds of small green parrots that frequented the area, screeching as they whirled, then settled, then took off again among the tall oaks. Their deafening shrieks and noisy chatter were so loud that lessons often had to be suspended until they had passed out of hearing, an interim that sometimes lasted several long minutes. It was annoying (to teachers, not us) if they remained in the trees nearby instead of going on, for then their raucous cries and socializing continued until the whistle blew and class was dismissed.

In October, when school began for the entire student body (the winter pupils did not arrive before then), we battled one of nature's less welcome wonders. Clouds of newly hatched black mosquitoes descended on Miami when the west wind from the Everglades blew, to be met by our choking smudge pots. These were metal cans that held fires fueled by rags and pine needles, the resulting thick, gray haze making breathing difficult for us and not discouraging the mosquitoes to any perceptible degree. To sit at a front desk in Miss Mary Bird Clayes' class required fortitude and an unflinching smile, for the Egyptian fly-switch she had acquired on her travels was brought into play, and the sting on our ankles from that flicking dried grass was about the same as that delivered by the hungry mosquitoes.

While we waited for fogging machines to be invented, we devised our own diversionary tactics. Since these pests (Did you know only the females bite?) sometimes covered the screens so thickly it was hard to tell whether or not there was a light on inside a room, we learned a little dance to avoid letting them into our habitats. Before entering any building, we quickly began vigorous stamping, slapping, whirling, and brushing of clothes and hair (not unlike today's stomp and rap moves), for these insects' *modus operandi* was to hide in the folds of clothing or in hair and be smuggled inside. Then followed a mad dash after shouts of "Ready?" signaled all was clear. It was not at all unusual to have the door slam shut so quickly after that desperate rush that clothing or an elbow did not always make it through in time.

Along with our unique open-air classrooms came an open-air theater. The stage was grass; a few white, wooden columns strung with lights marked the rear; a hidden piano sounded the accompaniment for our vocal efforts; and mercilessly bright footlights made everyone look like a ghost. No make-up, though, stage or otherwise, was allowed. My mother once furtively dabbed a little watered-down Mercurochrome on my lips so she could pick me out of the pale-faced chorus. Seemingly unavoidable bad luck with rainy weather often crowned these plein air events, its inevitability becoming an inside joke with students and parents.

There, on our grassy stage, we performed operettas written by Miss Harris, with musical accompaniment by Professor Andre (hidden in the shrubbery). Since the whole Lower School had to have parts, our performances were usually rife with fairies, pirates, and pajama girls. The stage also featured Santa Claus, who arrived each year just before dismissal for Christmas vacation. He supposedly came by boat from the bay, a daring innovation for pupils from the North. Where were his reindeer? they wondered. Could they swim? Shouldering his red pack full of presents, bells jingling promisingly, he emerged from the warm, jasmine-scented darkness into those glaring footlights, *ho-ho-ho*ing through his long, white beard. Was it Mr. White this year, or Mr. Rosser?

In late April, complete with unsigned diplomas awaiting final test scores, graduation exercises were staged for those Northern parents and friends whose luggage was already packed, ready to leave our steadily warming days. The snowbirds, we called them. Dr. Soper, greatly beloved pastor of St. Stephen's Church in Coconut Grove (who kept a monkey, Mickey, and two macaws as pets at his home), officiated, his white cassock flapping in the breeze from the bay. Miss Harris, soft, white hair crowning her erect figure, was dressed in her customary diaphanous, Isadora Duncan–style dress of white chiffon crepe, white hose and shoes, and blue agate beads to match the noted blue eyes. (These garments also came in various pastels, supplied by the school dressmaker.) The seniors, full of themselves in long, white dresses (checked for modesty) and carrying bouquets of red roses,

Nighttime graduation with seniors, flower girls, and Miss Harris.

each holding the hand of her small flower girl with her little basket of flowers, took the stage. "As we are you once were . . .," went their song, written by Miss Harris herself. As the final words echoed by the remaining student body— "Farewell voices soft are saying their goodbye to you . . ."— drifted out over the flower-perfumed air of the spring evening, graduates and their families rendezvoused for the last official event of the school year, though final exams still lay ahead.

In the 1920s and early '30s, Miami was a town with no symphony, art museums, or opera groups, and Miss Harris was mindful of the need to offer culture in some form in an environment where it was in short supply. One source that presented itself was the number of winter-visiting writers and artists looking for new patrons, new ideas, or just a quiet retreat in a warm place in which to create. They were often recruited by newly opened hotels and land developments for the publicity they generated. One Miamian told me the thrill of his life occurred when, at the tender age of five, he was dressed in his little, white linen suit and taken by his father to see Gilda Gray do the "shimmy" at the Venetian Pools, the outdoor "stage" where William Jennings Bryan

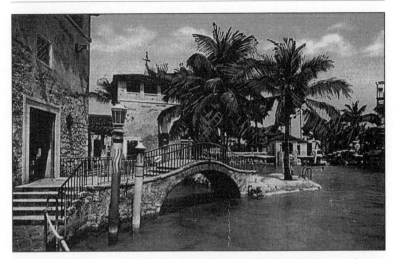

Once a rock quarry excavated for building materials, the Venetian Pool was transformed into outdoor swimming grottos and a stage.

extolled real estate and Paul Whiteman entertained. (Bing Crosby was a young unknown with the Whiteman orchestra then). This, of course, would not have been the choice of Miss Harris, but there were certainly many other well-known and more serious celebrities in the area.

One highly encouraged (though not very popular) event during the school year was the broadcast each week of the Damrosch Concerts for Upper School students assembled on the bayside lawn. Walter Damrosch, noted impresario of the NBC Symphony Orchestra, conducted his radio concerts for the enlightenment of the musically deprived through national broadcasts, known as the Music Appreciation Hour. Sitting outdoors on rugs or blankets, on terrace steps, and in deck chairs (each student had her own personal chair and, with many pinched fingers, eventually mastered the art of setting it up), we listened to the concertos and symphonies directed at us from a huge radio amplifier. This instrument was placed on a table next to Miss Harris, seated in her green wicker armchair on the veranda. From this slightly raised vantage point, she could clearly observe us morphing into music lovers. We were supposed to be answering questions in the little quiz texts distributed

Taking class with Miss Harris in our deck chairs.

to us each week, but it was mostly a time for giggling, passing notes, daydreaming, and getting a better tan in the sun
filtering through the palm fronds.

Noted guests sometimes showed up at our daily assembly. In addition to Ruth Bryan Owen, Robert Frost, who win-
tered in South Miami, visited us. On one memorable occasion, the shaggy-haired poet read his wonderful poem
"Stopping by Woods on a Snowy Evening." It was a thrill to
have the poet who had written what was in our schoolbooks
read his own work for us. Another day, there was a visit from
Sigmund Spaeth, known on national radio as the Tune
Detective, who accompanied himself on the piano and
showed us how one tune borrowed from another. A glimpse
of worldly sophistication of a sort reached us another morning in the form of a little talk delivered by the brother of a
classmate, recently returned from a year at Oxford on a
Rhodes Scholarship. He described for us some of the noble
traditions of that venerable university and how each student's room was assigned a valet. One of the man's duties,
he told us, was to bring a copper basin of hot water up three
flights of stairs every morning for shaving and bathing purposes. I don't know whether having a valet or not having

running hot water impressed us the most!

The most fascinating visitor, by far, was Mrs. Frank Gannet, wife of the publisher and mother of a classmate. She had written a book about life in the circus and to that end had traveled as an observer with the Big Top. We came away with tidbits of information about the superstitions, the animals, the clowns, and a firm resolve never to take the top slice of bread at the tented dining tables. That, it appeared, was reserved for the flies!

Those in the public eye who did not come to us could often be seen at the White Temple Church downtown, where sleepy-eyed Lower and Upper School girls stayed up past bedtime to listen to artists such as the world-renowned Ignatz Paderewski, who made the walls resound with his marvelous piano renditions. His performance was an inspiration or a discouragement, depending on whether you were still mired in scales and "Twinkle, Twinkle, Little Star." Famous tenor John McCormick, star of worldwide concerts and of classical favorites found on many Victrola turntables of the era, displayed his magnificent voice at the church. And one memorable afternoon, in a room at The Biltmore Hotel in Coral Gables filled with no more than seventy people, a young Carl Sandburg, dressed in checkered shirt and ankle-top country boots and crowned by the familiar shock of white hair, played his guitar, sang, and recited his well-known poem "Fog." I'm not sure those of us who were young and restless truly appreciated what we were experiencing.

The arts were on campus too. Professor Andre, a gentle giant of a man who had studied in Germany to be a concert pianist, encouraged a strong, dynamic touch on the keys. During one vigorous lesson, in fact, he hit a bass note so hard the string popped like a rifle shot, bringing people running to see what was the matter. On another occasion he attacked his instrument with such ferocity, the piano bench collapsed under him. "Vot iss?" he asked from his position on the floor. That was dynamism to his satisfaction. I can still hear his admonitions during those difficult lessons in muscle building—"Don't tickle the keys, please" and "No composing, please. Play what is written"—all delivered in his heavy German accent. Despite these valuable instructions, there was not, unfortunately, a Vladimir Horowitz or Myra Hess among us. One day, in a moment of exasperation, he told us that as a boy in Cologne, *his* teacher, at the first wrong note, had delivered a sharp smack to his knuckles with a ruler kept handy for the purpose, and if there was a second error in the lesson he was sent packing with his music. And his father had to pay the teacher anyway. Absorbing this lesson as well, we counted ourselves lucky to get away with as many mistakes as we made.

Mr. Rosser taught violin, an instrument that only begins to sound good with advanced students. Originally from England, with a personality and physique as taut as a violin string, he perhaps wore earplugs to deaden some of the screeches that came from the music room. In any case, his was not a popular instrument. You certainly couldn't play "The Music Goes 'Round and 'Round" or "The Lady in Red" on it properly, something all piano students tried on their Steinways.

Swiss artist Jean Jacques Pfister was our painting and art teacher who was noted for having painted a portrait of Mary Baker Eddy for the Mother Church of Christ Scientist in Boston (I believe it's still there). His very moving rendering of Charles Lindbergh's plane, *The Spirit of St Louis*, on its flight to Paris through the fog, entitled *We*, was ultimately reproduced on posters and enjoyed great national popularity at the time.

He was the perfect picture of an artist from the days of Rosetti or Sargent, with his frock coat, flowing gray hair under a soft fedora, and sharp, beaky nose. Mr. Pfister (his name had a nice rhyming quality) had been in San Francisco during the Great Fire, when, he said, from the hilltop where people huddled to watch the unbelievable destruction, the light was so intense you could read a newspaper in its glow. From there he traveled the West, painting landscapes—huge

*Artist Jean
Jacques Pfister as
a young man in
San Francisco.*

Beirstadt-like canvases of the Rockies, which reminded him
of Switzerland—then down into Louisiana, where the
swamps with their knobby-kneed cypress trees inspired
many misty, silvery gray paintings. These were especially
favored in Miami Beach's tropical homes, with their light or
pastel-colored walls, and the list of his patrons grew. Finally,
he took up residence in a studio in the Douglas Entrance in
Coral Gables, where he painted portraits in an easy style that
captured the sitter's likeness without offending.

I loved his classes. They were small and unstructured,
and his experience and encouragement kept his budding
artist students coming back each year (to say nothing of
the day he held our attention by relating how he and his
sisters made Swiss cheese with large, sticky bubbles in a

huge cauldron in Switzerland).

Dance was offered by a flurry of Isadora Duncan–type teachers—I cannot recall the many names—swathed in filmy chiffon in rainbow colors sashed over matching bloomers and shod in beige Dundeer sandals. Scarf dances and expressive, freeform movements were the bon ton of the day. The school filmed home movies of these efforts. Seeing these run backwards at high speed provided hilarious amusement for a long time.

For a school that offered both a curriculum and an atmosphere rather advanced for their day, there were some inexplicable courses of action. One was the mystifying addition on every monthly bill of fifty cents for water and paper cups. Granted, the water was bottled Tripure (rather like today's Evian), but this charge so upset parents, who felt tuition should cover a few cups of water, it was quickly removed. Another incident arose from a billing dispute with the Florida Power and Light Company. When it could not be resolved, Miss Harris installed her own generators, leading to a splurge of lights that burned needlessly night and day. Even bulbs in musty closets stayed lit, and the lamps at the school entrance were always blazing, rain or shine. In the end, Miss Harris' response to the electric company enabled her to use as much electricity as she pleased. It was a rare lost battle for Florida Power and Light.

Though Miss Harris' School was an institution that attracted curiosity (often tinged with a hint of—could it be?—envy) and criticism for its policies, its students loved it in spite of all its regulations. Those who preferred the coed student body of public schools and freedom from dress codes wondered how we managed. But there was a reason behind those rules. Uniforms and a lack of jewelry or make-up (a bottle of polish remover was kept in the office for those who dared to wear painted nails to class) allowed students from disparate family incomes to be equal. The focus was on the individual and her own efforts. Lack of artifice in those surroundings was admired. And not having the opposite gender on campus gave students a level playing field and freer social situations in which to mature. An institution like Miss Harris' School probably could not survive in today's culture of ego.

This was where I spent my school days during the 1930s. The feeling of being free and happy and content with one's small world is a memory I cherish to this day. But the times were moving on, and in the early 1950s, as Miami geared for post-war changes, such detachment from the outside world was no longer possible.

When downtown began marching southward, and the Ocean Reef Bar opened on South Bayshore Drive and SE 12th Street, and Channel 6 occupied a strange, round building next door known locally as "The Wallace Collar" building (where one could sometimes see the Red Baron, a television character in a red cape, jump into his silver car and tear off), Miss Harris decided it was no longer a neighborhood for the daughters of the families she wished to attract. So the property was sold, the school moved up the coast to Stuart, and a particular sphere of influence in Miami was gone forever.

they occupied was the envy of many.

Artist Louis Comfort Tiffany and his family had a home there, next door to the one later occupied by Mrs. Andre Rickmers, sister of Hervey Allen, author of *Anthony Adverse,* rage reading of its time. Today the sprawling concrete of the condominium development called Brickell Place occupies that address. Arthur Brisbane, whose national column for Hearst's *Chicago Tribune* made his byline familiar to thousands, lived where the Assumption Academy later opened its doors. The academy itself is no longer there, but the little church of St. Jude, built as a chapel for the school, still sits at the corner of Brickell and 15th Road. The heads of the First National Bank of Miami and the Bank of Bay Biscayne chose Brickell Avenue as their address. (The Bank of Bay Biscayne numbered among the bank failures of the 1930s, causing its president to flee the wrath of angry depositors.).

Around the corner on Point View (now called Brickell Bay Drive) was the home of Augustus E. Staley, founder of Staley Starch, which later became part of Beatrice Foods. It was a large, white house with a heavy, tiled roof and dark trim. Inside, dark paneling covered the walls. Tall, Tiffany stained-glass windows brightened the somber, old-fashioned interior of the breakfast room. Across the lawn from the main house, an entertainment annex, with a huge bar and dance floor and murals of Havana nightlife painted on the walls, waited for the next party. A three-car garage with servants' quarters above, built when many people did not hope to own a car, completed the home's amenities. It faced the bay, a view that included the large yachts conveniently moored for the winter at the private dockage at the front doors of Point View homes. Years later, the Staleys' granddaughter, songwriter and music arranger Shirley Cowell, bought her own house on Sunset Island from Howard Hughes. She said it had electrical and communication wires protruding from all of the walls, their purpose unknown to all but Howard Hughes and his entourage.

In some of the bayfront mansions, money and fantasy

POINT VIEW AND BISCAYNE BAY, MIAMI, FLA.

Very early view of Point View, now built solid with condominiums.

combined to provide every amenity for and satisfy every desire of the owners. In these pleasure palaces, one might find a ballroom for private parties. Or a tower music room, isolated from daily household activities, where one could enjoy the sounds of Bach or popular music along with panoramic views out four walls of windows. Some houses offered an elevator or two guest powder rooms, one for ladies, the other for gentlemen. A salon devoted entirely to an enormous electric train model, complete with its surrounding villages, mountains, and figurines, was just one of many surprises. Numerous bedrooms or separate guesthouses implied that overnight guests were an expected part of social life. It was an era when people entertained largely at home, not in clubs or hotels, and prized their privacy.

Drive down to Point View today and you'll see only a wide sidewalk above the sea wall. No trim, white and mahogany yachts ride the gentle swells that slap against the concrete. Instead of the pleasant winter homes that once housed prominent residents like the Staleys, the Milners of the Michigan hotel chain, and first *Miami Herald* publisher

Frank Shutts, the windows and miniature balconies of condominium high-rises overlook the promenade. Their mono-
lithic presence, cast in stolid, charmless concrete, chokes
land that once boasted graceful casuarinas and was often
subject to four- to five-foot floods during hurricanes. The
water sometimes covered Brickell Avenue itself.

Once, estates like these extended along Brickell from
15th Road as far south as the north wall of Vizcaya (US 1 did
not cut through to Key Biscayne). Sadly, the bayfront homesteads, from 15th Road south to the approach to
Rickenbacker Causeway, are all gone now. Along the way they
were exchanged for vertical living and a pared-down lifestyle.
Instead of the butler at the door, a doorman now answers for
all the residents. Only the remaining short cul-de-sac of
Brickell Avenue still has a few from that era. Sylvester
Stallone's house, now with a newer owner, an eight acre estate
built by the Deering heirs (builder of Vizcaya), which bore
the name "Casa Rocky" over its entrance archway during his
short residency, is there, as well as Madonna's former house
with canvas over its iron gates, just the feathery tips of the row
of royal palms lining the drive visible, hiding the long vista of
the house on the bay.

The last of the bayfront homes to go was the Santa
Maria estate, once home to the parents of Mercedes Ferre,
wife of Maurice Ferre, a former mayor of Miami. Her father,
a noted architect in Venezuela, designed the beautiful
Army/Navy Polo Club there. The Santa Maria condominium
rises today behind the original arched gateway, its once-
grand proportions now insignificant in the shadow of the
development it marks.

A large, two-story home of Spanish design, luxuriously
simple and inviting, Santa Maria was the setting one year for
a buffet dinner given by the Beaux Arts group of the Lowe
Gallery to thank their many donors and patrons. On that
balmy evening, the picturesque well in the courtyard was
filled with golden mums; red clay pots of the flowers lined
the tops of walls and narrow paths; candlelit tables were set

in the indoor patio; and a classical guitarist entertained guests with music from the heart of Spain as they dined on *arroz con pollo* with black beans (considered exotic in those halcyon days), green salad, and sliced Valencia oranges.

The evening became even more memorable when Maurice Ferre and his father, emerging from the darkness in authentic gaucho costume, rode their purebred Arab mounts up the drive and into the courtyard to greet the guests, the heavy, embossed silver on their black leather stirrups and saddles glinting in the moonlight. A very romantic sight.

6

*J*ewels in the Town

Vizcaya, Villa Serena, Indian Spring, et al.

izcaya. The very name breathes the romance of the Mediterranean sun, warm winds from Africa, and distant horizons. James Deering, an heir, along with his brother, to the International Harvester industrial fortune, built this private estate in 1916, importing artists and furnishings from Europe to create one of the finest private houses in America. It was always a rather secluded, heavily wooded property, its magnificent, wrought-iron gates always closed and the thick, dark green plantings behind them obscuring the pleasures that lay beyond. The faded pink containing wall, incised with geometric designs, ran past where Mercy Hospital now stands (on land given by the Deering heirs). That wall, topped by long, looping swags of brilliant bougainvillea, chalice vine, or bright yellow allamanda blooms, always signaled for me that we were now headed toward Coconut Grove. The property inevitably became an object of curiosity, a fiefdom outsiders could only speculate about. Tales of the beauty of its Italian gardens, lavish parties, and frequent visits by people in show business for the amuse-

40

M-281 VILLA VISCAYA, MIAMI, FLORIDA

Aerial view of Vizcaya and gardens.

ment of Mr. Deering's guests invited much attention from local residents. (Lillian and Dorothy Gish, friends of Vizcaya's architect, Paul Chalfin, visited often.)

So much has been written about this extraordinary house—its name, its setting, its furnishings, and history—there is little more to add. But one story that found its way to local gossip concerned a small house on the property, perched by the water a little distance from the main house, where James Deering was said to entertain his male guests. A man who had the good fortune to visit on occasion as a child recalled that any children on the premises were always sternly warned not to set foot on the path to the door of that little house. And children who often visited the family of Charles Deering, James's half-brother, who lived on an estate farther south, received a curious admonition—be good and one got to go to the Charles Deering home on Old Cutler; be naughty and one had to dress up in a little velvet suit and go to Vizcaya. Punishment indeed!

Once, when I was quite small, Vizcaya, with its stone ship breakwater, was opened to the public for one day only. It must have been for some charity benefit, though I cannot recall the exact purpose of this special event. Of course, everyone who could go did go. The estate had been closed for a few years, and, as I remember, the grounds were overgrown and neglected and repairs were needed here and there But the beautiful tiles and marble had kept their color (one visitor was recording those delicate tints in watercolor), and the vastness of the rooms still had the power to impress. Even the bathhouse, with its solid silver fixtures, and the gardens cultivated with plants from different parts of the world (the African Garden, the Chinese Garden) stimulated the imagination and were proof that the owner's attention to detail extended well beyond the house. Except for the chiggers picked up from the piles of unraked and moldering leaves beside the drive as we walked to our car afterward, it was a wonderful glimpse of the sophisticated lifestyle that informed our growing mélange of ideas.

Not open to the public that day was the property across the avenue, the working side of Vizcaya and the source of certain provisions for the main house when Mr. Deering was in residence. Modeled after many Italian estates, it provided a house for the property manager and his family. Within its walled acres were the gardens that yielded flowers to decorate the beautiful interiors of the main house; orange and grapefruit groves; and the confines where hen houses and pens of small animals were kept. There, too, were the seven-car garage, a paint shed for maintenance, and a barn for a horse and wagon (to bring water in case of fire at Vizcaya).

In the 1940s, Col. Harold Lewis, former West Pointer and Army man, lived in the property manager's house with his family, managing the estate for the heirs of James Deering for many years. Among the citrus groves, Lewis, a keen hunter since his boyhood in Arkansas, trained the hounds he raised to retrieve game on hunting trips. In 1959, when the property was purchased by Dade County, it was made available to the Museum of Science through Lewis's strong encouragement. He is remembered by a rose garden, named for him, at Vizcaya.

Beaux Arts held its annual costume ball at the residence in 1952, the first year Vizcaya was open to the public. In that magnificent setting, under a full moon, the past came alive. The lawns, dotted with small white tents and heraldic banners emblazoned in saffron, rose, and dark blue with the insignias of Italian noble families, became a fantasy stage. Jugglers, mimes, acrobats, and guests in elaborate Renaissance costumes, sated with fabulous food and exhilarated by music from strolling players, reveled in the illusion of the occasion. Guests reached the end of a perfect evening by sitting on the coral rock terraces that faced the darkened bay and stone ship breakwater. From there they watched glorious fireworks that sent great, golden showers of light high over the water, past endless bursts of fiery red and blue stars. The magic of that moment at Vizcaya will always overshadow any later visits for me. In my mind, that was Vizcaya at its very best.

North of Vizcaya on the bay side, at 3115 Brickell Avenue, is Villa Serena, a historic property that was once the residence of one-time presidential hopeful William Jennings Bryan and

Villa Serena, the home that once sheltered William Jennings Bryan, Mrs. William Matheson, and the William F. Cheek family.

his invalid wife, and later the residence of Mrs. William Matheson, matriarch of the pioneer Coconut Grove family.

In the 1930s, the house was purchased by William F. Cheek for his family. It is a large, white, two-story house, its twin wings forming a U shape in the front. It had the unusual feature of two separate but identical stairways to the upper story just inside the front entrance. Colorful, glazed tile dressed in beautiful Oriental rugs covered the floors then, and just beyond, unparalleled views of the open bay to the east could be seen from all rooms. The kitchen was, incredibly, all stainless steel—countertops, sinks, and appliances—and was large enough and complete enough for a restaurant. On the first floor, a beautiful, paneled library was the favorite room of Mr. Cheek, who spent most of his afternoons there, poring over his extensive and valuable stamp collection and the antique documents he collected.

Short in stature, gray-haired, a very cordial but taciturn man, William was a descendant of Joel Cheek, founder of Maxwell House Coffee, from Nashville, Tennessee. He and his wife lived at Villa Serena in quiet seclusion, contributing in many ways to the community and leaving more active pursuits to their children. The property offered tranquility and beauty—it was, indeed, a serene villa, as its name so aptly implied. On the bay side lay that sheer, seventeen-foot cliff of ridged limestone that dropped straight to the water. Off the front drive, hidden by crotons, gumbo limbos, and oak trees, stood a tall, screened gazebo where exotically plumaged pet macaws preened their stunning red, green, blue, and yellow tail feathers, some several feet in length. Squirrels kept the parrot seeds in view, and numerous butterflies—black and yellow zebras, orange and bronze monarchs, and swallowtails with their elegant tails (I miss them in today's Miami)—fluttered over the native plants.

One of the Cheek daughters told of watching sightseeing boats cruising by her residence as their passengers viewed waterfront estates, an activity still popular today. She was curious to know what was being said but had never taken the cruise. One summer afternoon, when the wind was right, the boat with its tourists came in to sight and she heard the captain on his megaphone, loud and clear. He announced, to her great astonishment, that at that moment they were passing the home of a man so rich, his children came down to breakfast each morning and looked under their plates to find a gold coin. "I wish," she said ruefully.

Next door to the Cheeks was the Stanley Joyce house, now called Indian Spring. It had once housed under its sloping roof a famous showgirl of the day, Peggy Hopkins Joyce, celebrated for her looks, for her jewels, for having married six times, and little else. When she and her then-husband, Chicago lumber millionaire James Stanley Joyce, bought the house, it became home to a number of free-roaming monkeys. Exotic animals were popular as pets in the 1920s. Ocelots, honey bears, and even curly-tailed kinkajous were a nice counterpoint in photographs of their glamorous owners, but monkeys and parrots did best in the tropics. And much to the annoyance of neighbors, their food supply grew in every garden.

Low and heavily landscaped, the home, whose double-wing floor plan was similar to that of Villa Serena, was rather undistinguished from the outside. But it had one curious feature (besides the monkeys)—a "crooky" court. A game similar to croquet but much more difficult to play, crooky is actually the ancestor of modern croquet. It originated in Ireland in the 1830s, later gaining popularity in England because it could be played by both men and women to equal advantage.

Seemingly a combination of croquet and billiards, crooky was certainly different in many ways from today's game. Instead of the expected green lawn, for instance, players used a permanent, small-gravel court that had to be rolled, a cement curb surrounding its rectangular playing area. Heavy, iron wickets allowed only one quarter inch of clearance for the wooden balls. Mallets and balls were slightly smaller than the ones we know today as standard. In any case, the game was far too complex for the beginner, which is probably why one doesn't see a lot of crooky courts today.

To the north of Indian Spring is the one we know today as Madonna's house at 3029 Brickell. Long before the arrival of that icon of outrageousness, the Howells built their dream home atop this bluff on the bay. Harry Howell, a ruddy-faced, self-made man with a strong cockney accent—made even more difficult to understand by the half-smoked cigar always in his mouth—spent his afternoons downtown watching the tickertape at the stock exchange offices. A bad day in the market increased his ruddiness by several degrees, reduced his speech to grunts, and resulted in a chewed as well as smoked cheroot.

Howell had started out in Miami in the early 1920s as a young salesman for James Bright, developer of Hialeah Race Track, and Glenn Curtiss, aeronautical engineer and developer of Miami Springs, selling land in a brand-new development called Hialeah. Lot prices began at $8. Howell was very good at selling, and, having made money in real estate in the boom years (and kept it), he built his beautiful house next to the older estates that lined the cul-de-sac at the end of Brickell Avenue.

Fit for a Spanish grandee, the house featured highly polished, hexagonal floor tiles of oxblood red in all the rooms on the ground floor and high ceilings of hand-painted, wooden beams that spanned the long, sunken living room and allowed bay breezes to circulate in the cool, dark interior. Five-foot-tall, black wrought-iron gates separated the living room from the elevated dining room, whose long windows faced east. Outside, centered on the terrace, a pale gray, semi-circular dance patio of polished stone overlooked the bay. Here, at afternoon tea dances, which were extremely popular then, guests found a smooth and elegant surface for waltzes, tangos, and fox trots beneath palms that swayed right along with them.

Like its neighbor Villa Serena, this luxurious property sat high above the water, with stairs cut into the limestone descending to a grassy landing by the sea wall. Built to last, the house had poured-concrete floor beams over a seven-foot-high crawlspace that allowed workmen who needed to go under the house to stand upright. In the entrance foyer, a curved, cut-keystone, coral staircase carpeted in pale green wool ascended in easy steps to landings with small, arched windows. The view from these was the long, straight front drive, along which a double line of lofty royal palms, with their green fronds and swollen, silvery gray trunks, marked the approach from the front gate.

Such grandness seemed to be a constant responsibility weighing heavily on Mrs. Howell, a petite, Australian native with a lilting accent. Smiling and dainty, she was constantly in motion, fastidious and fussily tidy. In spite of three servants, who were replaced frequently since they always seemed to be at odds with one another, she sometimes ended up answering the door herself in cleaning apron and gloves, wisps of fluffy, blond hair escaping from an old scarf on her head.

I remember that Shalimar, so evocative of 1920s' taste, was Mrs. Howell's favorite perfume, and a huge, cut-crystal flask of it always sat on her dressing table. In my memory, that soft, exotic scent, emanating from the pale blue master bedroom, spoke of happy times and imminent, grown-up parties. It can still bring back reminders of a time when people were not always too busy pursuing a career, or incessantly traveling for short trips here and there, but rather savoring a more leisurely existence. When dressing exquisitely was accepted form and an afternoon of bridge was nothing to feel guilty about. When a box at the races for the afternoon was not a tax write-off but pure entertainment with friends whose company you enjoyed.

Everything changed, of course, with the advent of World War II. Big houses were hard to maintain. Help was scarce, electric and fuel consumption curtailed. Suddenly, smaller was better. Beyond that, Harry Howell, like many, thought Miami property values would go down after ominous reports of Nazi subs off our shores shook Americans' complacency. So the Howells sold their home for $80,000 and left for California. None of their fears materialized, however, and years later, Madonna paid nearly $5 million for that address, a fact that bothered Mr. Howell for the rest of his life. Location, location, location! Today, public records show the property has been purchased for $7.5 million by a dog, a noble-looking German shepherd whose deceased owner, it has been loudly publicized, left it a bequest of $150 million. Only in Miami!

Following World War II, the Francis (Mike) Calhouns bought the Howell house. They hung a huge Baccarat chandelier, taken from a Miami Beach hotel that was being razed, above the stairwell of the cut-keystone stairs. It was a little scary to walk under the chandelier, which was so heavy it had to be hoisted to its location. The interior decor became a mix of contemporary furnishings, Austrian shades, and mounted animal heads and antlers on the library wall. A pool was added next to the dance patio outside, with cherub fountains at each corner. Plantation shutters even appeared at the windows. The house became an Italian villa, painted an intense terra cotta that was supposed to fade.

The property's claim to fame in the annals of Miami history came during the Calhouns' residency, when Barbara Mackle was abducted. Barbara was the daughter of one of the prominent Mackle brothers, owners of the Deltona Company and developers of Key Biscayne, Marco Island, and other well-known resort destinations in Florida. In the fall of 1968, she and her mother were awaiting the end of her college mid-semester exams in an Atlanta motel when she was kidnapped. Her abductors delivered their ransom demands, naming a deadline for the payoff in Miami. The resulting interstate manhunt by the police, the FBI, and private detectives hired by the family failed to locate either the girl or her abductors. As time drew near for the ransom to be collected, with no assurances that Barbara was still alive, the frustration and fear for her safety grew steadily. Although the girl's family was determined to comply with her abductor's demands, the search for her continued, everyone hoping for a break in the case.

It came in a most unexpected way. One night, according to a friend of the Calhouns, a sleepless Mike Calhoun stood at the window of his upstairs bedroom, looking out toward the bay, and noticed something strange. A small boat had pulled up to the shore of the vacant, wooded property to the north. A single figure jumped out and disappeared into the darkness of the mangroves. Local police were notified of the prowler, but a security force sent to scour the grounds found no one. Unbeknownst to the press and general public, however, this figure was the kidnapper, following the agreed-upon plan for delivery of the ransom. The resulting hue and cry scared the man off, causing the ransom drop to be aborted, a serious problem with time running out. The delivery had to be planned anew.

On the second attempt, the ransom money ($500,000 in old twenties) was left at the designated location. Barbara Mackle was released unharmed from a coffin that had been buried on a pine-covered hillside in Norcross, Georgia. For eighty-three hours, she had been buried underground, with a fan and small vent, just a few miles from the motel from which she had been taken. Amazingly, the courageous woman was in good physical and mental condition after her traumatic experience. Within a week, a young man and his female companion were captured on Florida's west coast as they tried to escape, and were charged with the crime.

A happy ending, but Mike Calhoun's insomnia very nearly spoiled it all.

7

*L*asting Impressions

Petit Douai

Brickell Avenue makes an elbow at 15th Road, a bend so dangerous it was often the scene of many an early-morning accident. Fortuitously, a doctor used to live on one corner of the street and an attorney on the other. The two professionals were accustomed to pulling on dressing gowns at the sound of sirens in the wee hours and finding someone who had partied too much sprawled on the parkway, his car trying to climb one of the coconut palms. The victim was sure to need either a doctor or a lawyer. When the two professionals decided which it would be, the other went back to bed.

From the 1920s until the end of World War II, this length of Brickell was considered exclusive, sometimes referred to as "Millionaire's Row." Some of the residents along the "Row" were prominent in their chosen fields and considered wealthy within their various circles. Some were perhaps even millionaires, a term that meant something then. They included Arthur Brisbane; Frank Shutts; the Staleys; the widow of Carl G. Fisher, an early developer of

Miami Beach; former Miami Mayor Everest G. Sewell (usually referred to as E. G.); members of the Louis Comfort Tiffany and Burdine families; and last, but by no means least, the aptly named minister, Dr. Angel.

The Brisbane house, a huge, three-story, bayfront home at the southeast corner of Brickell Avenue and 15th Road, later became the province of the Academy of the Assumption, a private school and convent. The school won its zoning acceptance in what was until then a totally residential area with the help of John and Sheelah Murrell and their neighbors' realization that Brickell Avenue was beginning to change. Later, the Catholic Order built the beautiful little chapel of St. Jude that still faces Brickell and 15th Road, a special amenity for those in the upscale neighborhood. A magnificently situated parcel of land, the original Brisbane property is today the footpad of the Villa Regina condominiums.

On the southwest corner of Brickell Avenue and 15th Road sits a house often noted by passersby for its unique architecture. Set on an eight-foot bluff above today's traffic, it is best described as a miniature French chateau. Called Petit Douai, it was built in 1930 on the lot once heavily filled with oaks at 1500 Brickell. Owners John and Ethel Ernest "Sheelah" Murrell were husband-and-wife attorneys, a rarity in those days. The house's architect was the firm of Kiehnel and Elliott, who also designed El Jardin (now Carrollton School) in the Grove, as well as the English Tudor house across from El Jardin, both impressive residences. The English Tudor was named Cherokee Lodge, originally built for the sister of John Bindley, president of Pittsburgh Steel.

Inspired by Douai, the French family estate of a fellow student Sheelah visited when studying at the Sorbonne, Petit Douai, as she called her fantasy imitation, was built of gray stone, its high-pitched slate roofline and central tower banked by sharp-pointed dormer windows and French doors. It was a mysterious choice of style to neighbors more accustomed to Mediterranean lines. They often referred to

*Petit Douai, home
of "that family that
lives in a church."*

the Murrells as "that family that lives in a church." Much curiosity centered, too, around Sheelah's Mexican hairless lap dog, Millicent. Not the most attractive breed in the canine world, having splotchy, pink skin and a topknot of hair, Millicent wore specially made silk pajamas to ward off sunburn—yet another topic of wonder to the neighbors.

Arthur Brisbane, the Murrells' neighbor across the street, was best known as an editorial journalist of the 1930s and former newspaper owner with connections to the Hearst publishing empire. It was with surprise that the Murrells opened their newspaper at breakfast one morning to read in Brisbane's column that their pet German shepherd, Spike, had trespassed, unbeknownst to his owners, onto the Brisbanes' premises and had made very short work of two of the fancy bantam roosters the Brisbanes kept as pets. Spike and his evil deed received the full attention of the entire column, a tirade berating people who didn't keep their pets chained and a special rebuke for Spike. Brisbane's outrage was plain for the entire country to witness. Needless to say, national embarrassment led to full and quick restitution. The prize bantams were replaced. Spike hung his head whenever the word "chicken" was uttered, and, until things settled down again, had to be content with retrieving coconut husks thrown off the sea wall at Point View.

At Petit Douai, where crenellated trim topped the garage roofline and servants' quarters to the rear, the Murrells' ten-year-old son played Robin Hood with his friends, shooting make-believe arrows through the openings and climbing the property's massive oak trees that were his fantasy Sherwood Forest. It was an easy stretch of the imagination, given the leafy boughs that hung over the point at Brickell. The largest one of those spectacular specimens went down in a hurricane in the 1930s, an all-too-often disaster in this area. Botanist Dr. David Fairchild was invited to assess the damage and the age of the upended old oak, whose roots saw the sky for the first time. In his opinion, it could have been there when Columbus landed in America.

Inside this Neo-Renaissance house with French pretensions, a cool, three-story hall looked straight up to the ceiling of a tower, from whose conical center hung an imposing, wrought-iron chandelier. Here and throughout the downstairs, the floor was tiled with large, imported, blue and gray square slabs of slate. A tall, antique pier glass graced one wall near a small fireplace. Tables from the Granada Crafts Workshop of the 1920s held handmade, iron candlesticks. A curved, wrought-iron stairway on the right, replete with marble steps, spanned a great height to the second story. On the left lay a long, sunny drawing room with its fireplace of white marble and pairs of French doors lining the walls on three sides of the room. Soffits concealed incandescent lighting behind classical plasterwork, lighting that washed the high ceilings with a warm glow.

From the foyer, with its heavy wooden door, one looked directly ahead to a half-flight of marble steps leading to the elegant dining room, which overlooked the pool area. A gracious, cream-colored room with gray-blue stone floors and exposed ceiling beams, it had often served to entertain guests from different parts of the world. Under a gracefully carved chandelier lay the long, polished dining table, covered in Venise lace and topped by a splendid, heavy centerpiece of Mexican silver. At the far end of the room, a built-in, marble-top buffet, surmounted by a tall, antique mirror, was bracketed by two narrow, stained-glass windows that admitted soft, colored light. French doors opened to a small, screened lanai that overlooked the garden, where cocktails were often served.

The dining room contains one of the seven fireplaces in the house. When the inordinate number of fireplaces was asked about, a cautionary family tale was repeated with a mixture of amusement and embarrassment. It seems that when the house was still under construction, Mrs. Murrell, walking through the litter and debris with the architect one afternoon, stopped before a fireplace being built, admired its effect in the room, and idly asked her adviser how much it cost. On hearing a reasonable figure mentioned, she indicated that it might be nice to have one in each of several other rooms. Certainly, one in each bedroom would be charming, she thought, and, of course, the den and library could not do without. After all, the thickness of the walls of this little chateau might need warming on cold days.

It was not until construction was completed and the bills presented that Sheelah Murrell learned the shocking truth. The architect had quoted a price for each mantel while she thought he had quoted the cost of an entire working fireplace. And that is why there are so many fireplaces in this Florida house, more than are really needed in such a temperate climate. Later, these hearths were shielded by hand-wrought, copper fire screens, each bearing a design by

Petit Douai today with encroaching high-rises in the background.

a different artist—a bow to the old adage "When you've got it (however acquired), you might as well flaunt it."

Before the house could be fully furnished, the Depression placed a moratorium on many people's plans. Instead of French-style pieces, which came later, the Murrells used massive Spanish tables and chairs turned out by the old Granada Furniture Workshop (which later became the site of the Charade Restaurant in the old Crafts Section of Coral Gables). Victorian suites arrived from Sheelah Murrell's family home in Wyoming. These latter formed their groupings with dignity but were oddly dwarfed by the twelve-foot ceiling in the drawing room and its grand piano. Years later, on Sheelah Murrell's death, that early furniture was returned to her home in Laramie (grateful to be back home in the West, no doubt), where there is a small museum exhibit celebrating pioneer families.

Though very feminine, Ethel Ernest Murrell was a strong feminist. She was born in Wyoming, the first state to give women the vote and to have the first woman governor. This undoubtedly influenced her outlook on the possibilities for women. A streak of independence may have come from her Irish grandfather, John Connor, who snowshoed from Laramie to Cheyenne in a snowstorm to record a deed to oil properties before another homesteader could stake the claim. The ranch lands and oil properties that her family owned eventually slipped away, but the Connor Hotel, long a downtown meeting place and the only hotel in Laramie, remained her property until her death. One of its visitors in the early 1900s was Teddy Roosevelt. On her dresser, Sheelah Murrell kept a photograph of herself at the age of four, a very poised and serious little girl sitting in the saddle with the Rough Rider himself on his horse during one of his hunting trips to Wyoming.

An only child whose grandparents had played a large part in Laramie's early history, Sheelah was doted on and spoiled, which made her unpopular in a little town where frontier sensibilities held sway. It showed in her manner—charming but always a little aloof until she felt she could trust a person. Then she was amusing and extremely intelligent but still brittle, not the most relaxing company. She traveled east to school, as many children of moneyed Western families did in those days, attending Chevy Chase in Washington, D.C. There, Sheelah's roommate introduced Sheelah to her brother, Ken Browning, whose Mormon father invented the Browning automatic rifle used by the U.S. Army in World War I and was later knighted in Great Britain for his achievement. Some years later, Sheelah married Ken Browning in a Mormon ceremony and moved to California.

That marriage ended shortly, and Sheelah met and married John Murrell, a recently widowed Miamian. With his early Miami partner, Senator Malone, he was Mary Brickell's attorney at the time and was building his practice as a young trial lawyer in the growing city. He was a gregarious Southerner who always stopped to greet friends (people in a hurry hated to walk down the street with him!). He encouraged his new wife to enter law school at the University of Miami, where she received her degree, a singular distinction at a time when many thought finishing schools enough education for a woman.

In the early 1930s, the gray chateau on the bluff at 15th Road became the setting for afternoon musicales with the composer Manna-Zucca at the piano; gatherings of the little, amateur theater group from the Coral Gables Country Club, of which the then-unknown Joseph Cotten was a member; and the kinds of teas and readings so popular in those days. John Murrell refused to attend any of these events. A man of strong opinion, he disapproved of "pantywaist poets" with their unfathomable, literary images, and his footsteps pacing overhead always gave a nervous edge to the readings.

Sheelah Murrell, in her turn, thoroughly enjoyed the creative ideas of others. She was an author herself, penning *The Golden Thread*, a treatise on comparative religions, and *Law for the Ladies*, a law primer for women. She also used her four-foot-deep, tiled tub in the master bedroom as a workspace where she amused herself modeling fanciful, clay masks to add to the collection in her wood-paneled den. A favorite of visitors was "Ranga," the gold-and-black Balinese mask whose long, red ribbon tongue was covered with tiny mirrors, the better to deflect evil.

But there were serious causes, too, that attracted her interest and support. The Soroptimists, for instance, an organization for women who owned their own businesses, met at the Murrells' house. The formation of the Soroptimists broke new ground in the 1930s, a time when women were not eligible for membership in the many organizations that helped business owners network (although one group of women formed the Committee of 99, a sly reference to the prestigious Committee of 100 for men). The Bay Oaks Home for the Aged was organized at 1500 Brickell Avenue as well, and the house's spacious, book-lined library, with its own entrance, was often used as an office for Sheelah's pro bono law practice.

John and Sheelah Murrell with guest at the Surf Club in the 1950s.

The most important work that took place in Petit Douai was the long and arduous campaign to change Florida law regarding the status of women. In the 1930s, married women in Florida were grouped with "orphans, idiots and chattels." The law was finally changed in 1943 after years of effort, and the most vociferous advocate of the Married Woman's Act was Ethel Ernest Murrell. Under the act's provisions, women were no longer classified as personal property. They no longer had to apply for a Free Dealership, or a legal change in status, in order to buy and sell their own property without their husbands' consent. They were, in short, entitled to equal rights with men. Still, some years later, Sheelah Murrell said she could not understand why more women did not take advantage of the new rights and freedoms that the law now afforded them. It took a long time for women to realize what doors had been opened for them.

Managing a large home and keeping up with career interests and social obligations often meant leaving many tasks to a team of trusted servants. If the residents along Brickell Avenue belonged to "Millionaire's Row," the people who served them belonged to "The Brickell and Bay Club," a group open by invitation only to those who were skilled enough to be employed in such prestigious surroundings. It may sound politically incorrect today, but back then servants took great pride in providing knowledgeable service. Servants were often considered family and remained for many years with the same household. Their virtues were loyalty and patience, as well as the ability to bear with good grace all the foibles of the families they served. They attended family weddings and funerals, tended to children, and gave continuity to the lives of their employers. Nothing like it today.

The Murrells employed a live-in couple as servants: a wizened, little black man named Senator Bailey and his wife, Sally. Small and neat in his starched, white jacket, the baldheaded Senator, ancient beyond time and Southern to the bone, was always referred to as Bailey, and there was a good reason for that. In his first year at 1500 Brickell, John Murrell, a man with many political friends, had surprised a visitor by calling for "Senator" to bring him a drink. The erroneous impression that a political lackey might be indentured was quickly erased by never referring to the man other than by his surname from that time onward.

The impassive Bailey took his duties as houseman at Petit Douai very seriously, but there were gaps in his understanding that came to light at odd moments. The Baileys were not always inclined to ask for clarification when orders were unclear. Perhaps they were unaware there were other ways of doing things, or perhaps they felt they should not bother their busy employers. In any case, they all too often made their own assumptions, which could sometimes lead to unpredictable results. Hardly a week went by without a new tale of misadventure from the houseman and his wife.

It was one of Bailey's responsibilities, for instance, to take the station wagon for grocery shopping, an excursion he always looked forward to, as he loved to chauffeur, his small, capped head barely visible above the steering wheel. One year, however, the results of his shopping expeditions seemed full of errors. Tomatoes, Bailey, not tomato sauce. Black beans, Bailey, not baked beans. With no explanation forthcoming, a little careful detective work was called for. It revealed that, like many of his generation, Bailey had never learned to read and was embarrassed to admit it. For years, in spite of that, he had managed very well by simply memorizing the shopping list and selecting the required items from pictures of the contents on the front of packages. Unfortunately for Bailey, though, many food companies had begun to redesign their labels to show only the name of the product and no picture, leaving him bewildered but disinclined to confess it. However, once his employers deduced the situation and the resulting impasse, they solved the problem by quietly turning to store deliveries. (But that cat was out of the bag.)

One spring evening during the Depression, a distinguished high court judge visiting from New Orleans, a city famous for its fine food, was a guest at dinner. In those days, steak was a special treat, and an entrée of prime steak had been planned as worthy of the visitor's gourmet palate. Bailey, entrusted with the preparation of this dish, first presented the perfectly done sirloin for his hostess' inspection. With a nod of approval, she told him to take it back to the pantry and slice it. In a few moments, the steak was proudly brought back by a beaming Bailey. However, to Sheelah Murrell's horror, the prime offering returned to the table split sideways—carved so that the rare center lay bleeding on the silver platter, its red juices puddling. This was just another reminder that one had to be very specific with Bailey.

Bailey's wife was much younger than he and towered over him, though her height did not give her any advantage in their arguments. A strong, big-boned woman with large feet and strange braids in her hair, she too was inclined to do things in her own way. The big, white kitchen in the house once had a primitive, built-in garbage receptacle, which Sally believed to be a newfangled dishwasher, a mistake that eventually called for a plumber and his bill. Both arrived in due time; the broken china and bent silver were retrieved; and the garbage convenience was removed forever.

Petit Douai still sits on that point of land, but the once-grand home has been turned into doctors' offices. The steps up to the dining room have been leveled, making the stained-glass windows that once framed the buffet into high clerestory openings, and a competent receptionist in a white nurse's uniform has replaced Senator Bailey in his white jacket.

8

W*ritten in Stone*

Coconut Grove, the Village

O
n South Bayshore Drive, trundling toward the village of Coconut Grove, large estates used to climb the rise to the west, a vantage point from which they could view the little boats and ever-changing colors of Biscayne Bay shimmering beyond their windows. Gracious homes lined the fringes of the bayfront where L'Hermitage villas and Grove Isle condos now house the affluent. In an active hurricane season, those who lived on the east side could expect to receive three or four feet of flooding from tidal surges alone, causing ruin to flooring, wallpaper, appliances, and any belongings left standing on the first floor. Properties situated to the west, on top of the coral ridge, avoided the flooding, but wind damage could be severe. In the wettest storms the bay sometimes advanced halfway up those ancient limestone cliffs, leaving numerous deep ridges on their face, still visible today, to mark the high-water levels. These grooves are a clear indication that the shore of the bay once ended at the foot of these porous gray bluffs, the land to the east evolving later from fill by nature or man. In those stone

hieroglyphs, riddled by constant decomposition of the soft rock, can be read the chronicle of storms that passed this way long before mankind moved into the area.

Where the Coral Reef Yacht Club docks its members' yachts and sailing craft, and nautical flags whip in the breezes off the water, a house that went from private ownership to private membership surveys the marine activity in its backyard. Once the home of an early Miami resident who lost everything in the years following the bust of the late 1920s, it had been built in 1922 for Clifford Cole, scion of the wealthy Cole family, maker of kitchen ranges. In the 1950s, it was the residence of George Engle, an entrepreneur with a penchant for speculation in oil wells. When Engle finally hit "black gold" in a large wildcat well in the dense swamps of Louisiana in the 1950s, it was a stroke of good fortune that freed him and his brother, Stanley, to try other projects.

Fond of the Grove and confident of its future, he turned his attention to the sleepy village to the south. He found a community satisfied with its cluster of small shops, churches, and hidden estates, more interested in its quiet way of life and the natural beauty it fiercely guarded than in the new conveniences being planned for it. The faithful Lyle's Pharmacy (now a branch of the Coconut Grove Bank); the Hamlet, a tiny, dark bar that was well populated night and day with regular patrons; the old watch-repair shop next door; and the hardware store with its rough, wooden floors had long been equal to most residents' needs, they reasoned.

Nevertheless, Engle proceeded to build the first new commercial building the Grove had seen for decades—the Engle Building, an ugly, gray, two-story brick edifice that blanketed the corner of Main Highway and McFarlane Road and still defines that crossroads. It also gave notice that the Grove's old way of life was about to change. Grovites warily noted the newcomer and the changes afoot. Since the days of its first settlers, denizens of the Old Grove had always embraced a philosophy of "live and let live," which was rarely abused, and had accommodated or tolerated newcomers with little comment (though they might have had their mental reservations). But this was something quite different. These coming changes were not meant to fit in but to overwhelm—in short, to challenge Coconut Grove's notable respect for individual ideas. What the residents were hearing, in fact, were the first faint notes of retreat. Unwanted, unsought, unadmired though these alterations might be, the Village was nevertheless about to feel the prosperity that would come from brash new shops, heavy traffic, tourist crowds, and sidewalk dining. The ticket price, it turned out, would be the loss of its quiet way of life in little byways and hidden coves, and a frenetic popularity that would eventually bring an end to the original look and feel of the Grove.

The Engle Building a *fait accompli*, George Engle then moved to acquire the Coconut Grove Theater from the Claughton family, owners of Claughton Island (today's Brickell Key), whose patriarch, it was said, had once served time for income tax evasion and was proud of it. The familiar old movie house that anchored the south end of the business district on Main Highway became the focus of the ambitious plan George Engle had in mind. This shabby structure from the 1920s, a time when Rococo plasterwork and fake balconies defined architectural tastes, was the Grove's only movie theater, a place where one could catch films whose age or lack of popularity had relegated them to the suburbs. Worn and tired from use and neglect and in sad need of major repair, its attractions were usually second-rate reruns and its audiences often a mere handful of viewers.

As well as the usual single seats, one row in the darkened interior had the only love seats that I can remember seeing in any theater. On hot summer nights in the 1930s, uniformed ushers with Flit guns patrolled the aisles during the show to keep away any pesky mosquitoes, lest their whining and the resulting slapping distract from the action on the silver screen or, worse yet, cause the audience to leave. Instead of air conditioning, a few large fans struggled against humid summer evenings. Sometimes the exit doors near the stage were left ajar during performances to catch any wayward breath of air, a practice that encouraged bugs, unpaid admissions, and even an occasional rat from the nearby alley to join the paying patrons.

In its stead, Engle envisioned a first-rate theater where Broadway plays could hold tryouts, established performers (such as Victor Borge) could give concerts, and new playwrights could showcase their efforts. Feeling the time was right to redress some of Miami's cultural deficiencies, he retained native Miamian Al Parker, a former student of Frank Lloyd Wright, to totally redo the property. The new plan would provide a stage suitable for live theater, the latest in acoustics and lighting, and, above all, comfortable new seats and air conditioning. It was a tremendous undertaking—subject to many struggles with the acoustics, which had to be redesigned several times—but in the end, a little jewel of a theater emerged. The site became the Coconut Grove Playhouse, sophisticated and luxurious, with the latest in stage equipment, a restaurant, and an upstairs reception area for celebrity cocktail parties and vernissages.

One of the new theater's first productions was Tennessee Williams' *A Streetcar Named Desire.* Tallulah Bankhead, a name that in those days resonated with star power and recognition, was cast as the pathetic Blanche Dubois. Williams himself, who often visited his sister Rose in Miami, came up from his home in Key West for opening night. The evening was a gala occasion, excitement and expectations running high. The audience was not disappointed. The performance was pure Tallulah, that famous drawl wringing every bit of self-drama out of the role, causing Williams to be heard to remark "That woman has ruined my play!" and leaving the audience impressed with the celebrities in attendance and with this new venture on their doorstep. Nightlife had come to the Grove, where dim streetlights and shuttered shops had formerly prevailed after sunset. George Engle had seen the future and, with a sure

Coconut Grove Playhouse after renovation. The premiere of Waiting for Godot *was held here.*

touch, had placed his bet correctly.

It was a tour-de-force run, during which Miss Bankhead stayed at George Engle's home (today's Coral Reef Yacht Club's clubhouse), though it is doubtful she brought her pet monkey. Gloria Swanson and Joan Bennett also stayed there during their appearances in subsequent plays, because, in those distant days, Coconut Grove had no hotel.

It also had no Catholic church, although there were many beautiful churches of other denominations in the area. Plymouth, St. Stephen's, and Bryan Memorial had been in their leafy settings for years, each so picturesque that people not of the congregation often chose to be married there because of the charming atmosphere. When St. Hugh's was finally designated a parish (with immeasurable help from the widowed Mrs. Hugh Matheson), the Coconut Grove Playhouse was used for Sunday morning Mass until the present church could be built. It was a strange sensation, indeed, for parishioners, who had trouble genuflecting before the curtained stage with its portable altar (and later had trouble

not genuflecting when they attended a theater performance). It was suggested by some that the huge fish pool in
the theater lobby be pressed into service as a baptismal font,
but I don't believe that was ever acted upon. The builders
for the new church just worked a little faster.

Father Ward, a Latin scholar and able priest given the
task of guiding this flock, soon found where Grovites' overriding interests lay. He once declared he had had so many
calls from Grovites about not destroying any of the banyan
trees that bordered the site for the new church, he wondered aloud if a lot of Druids lived there. He was probably
not far off the mark! On the completion of the Church of
St. Hugh, designed by architect William Tscheumy and constructed without the loss of a single banyan, the parishioners
moved into their more orthodox quarters, leaving the commercial area and the theatre behind.

After its brilliant start, the Coconut Grove Playhouse
seemed unable to maintain the lofty standards on which its
owner had set his sights. The premiere of Samuel Beckett's
new play, *Waiting for Godot*, was greeted by a mass exodus
up the aisles as less sophisticated theatergoers refused to sit
through the performance. The hope that live theater could
pay its way was eventually dashed when newer and larger
theaters opened on the Beach and downtown. Finally, the
playhouse was reduced to offering innumerable appearances
of the cult hit *Hair* to fill its seats.

With support for live shows dwindling, other ideas for
reviving the theater's popularity surfaced. An attempt at
state ownership, like that accorded the Asolo Theater in
Sarasota, failed. The Grove Art School next door—with
ceramic classes and a gallery of local artists, (Tony
Scornavaca and Gene Massin were in their heyday)—found
the burden of lending support too heavy and closed its
doors. And a valiant effort to keep its audience numbers up
by busing tourists from Miami Beach only cheapened its
original style. The tourists often became a show in themselves. Insecure about how to dress for the Grove and hav-

ing heard comments about the "far out" garb of its free-spirited inhabitants, they spilled off the buses arrayed in a curious
mixture of colorful beads, leisure suits, sandals, and pedal
pushers—none of which could disguise the obvious conclu-
sion that they were not genuine hippies. They deserved an "A"
for effort, though. (After all, most were over thirty.)

Other notes of change came when La Casita, a delightful
tearoom nearby that perfumed the air of Main Highway with
its aroma of fried chicken, eventually became the Taurus
Restaurant, with its aroma of grilled steak and wine, and a
more sophisticated Grove began to emerge. Waldo Perez
brought a touch of Palm Beach with the hand-painted door of
his interior design shop across from Bert's Groceteria. Even
Bert's, the high-end grocery emporium that specialized in
stocking yacht galleys, joined the rush to the new image by
introducing chocolate-covered bumblebees in tiny cans and
putting down plush blue carpet for its customers. The Grove
was packaging its charm—and depleting it.

It was still the Grove, of course, unlike any other part of
the city. Kresge's 5 & 10, where a child's allowance went as
far as next week, and the post office and the local liquor
store down the street still had a little life remaining. The
Christian Science Reading Room managed to keep its small
window on Main Highway, with its view of the streams of
flower children, hippies, freaks, druggies, tourists, and plain
folk who flowed past as the years counted new arrivals. But
a pleasant, laid-back way of life was fading into mythology,
and its spirit was being reinvented by every new visitor,
according to some inner vision, until it became increasingly
difficult to recall which lifestyle had brought everyone there
in the first place. Popularity was killing the Grove.

9

*B*etween the Leaves

Persons of Interest

Coconut Grove, older than Miami, was annexed by the city in the summer of 1925 when most of its residents were out of town and unable to vote. Always a little apart from its neighbors, both physically and in spirit, this edge of town has more than its share of interesting old houses secluded behind the high hedges of Surinam cherry or aralia, low rock walls, and the heavy green shrubs that line the winding lanes. The Grove invites pleasant walks and bicycling, gardening in sunny beds, or just sitting on benches in bowers of tropical leaves. Its look has caused many to describe it as almost English in atmosphere, and there is, agreeably, a sense of the same privacy and insularity that that comparison evokes.

Those individuals who naturally gravitated to the Grove from the very beginning were, for the most part, people with a strong sense of values (mostly liberal), a love of nature, and usually a soft spot for animals. From the early pioneers—those who fished for their food and caught turtles in the bay—to the wealthy estate owners who came later, an interesting blend of

architecture, gardens, and residents was forged. Small cottages
and charming hideaways with names like Plaisance and Chota
Khoti were often tucked next to large estates like Four Way
Lodge, now a subdivision of million-dollar homes. These modest dwellings were often where writers and artists pursued
their craft, with a retired Egyptologist or anthropologist somewhere in the mix for good measure. Since there is no profit in
trying to subdivide these small parcels, many have survived
and are much sought after today for their originality. But their
days are numbered.

The early Grove was a place where art and old money
existed comfortably side by side, their very different worlds
intact. Each party was curious about the other's way of life,
and there was always mutual respect. Often, deep friend-
ships that had no regard for fame or position were the result.
Your compatibility depended, in fact, more on the sort of
person you were.

Nature's gifts—flora, fauna, and the bay—were the glue
holding such diversity of residents together. Those gifts were
jealously protected from the anathema of developers' intru-
sive ways. And those gifts, so abundant in numerous secret
gardens filled with birdsong and bougainvillea, lizards and
fern, were carefully screened behind high hedges and
untrimmed trees. The uniquely rich soil in the old hammocks,
where ages of fallen oak leaves and ferns had made a loam that
favored whatever was placed in it, was a boon to the amateur
gardener. It also fostered many new species of plant life
brought from other parts of the world by travelers such as Dr.
David Fairchild. The world-famous botanist (and husband of
one of Alexander Graham Bell's daughters) had had a long
and distinguished career with the U.S. Department of
Agriculture before his retirement, and, over time, introduced
many non-indigenous plants to the grounds of his home on
Douglas Road, called The Kampong. Visited by students and
botanists from all over the globe, they continue to grow there
today—rough-skinned and bitter grapefruit as big as small
pumpkins, various species of bamboo, rare and curious fruits

and flowers. As our Bahamian yardman was fond of observing of plants that flourished: "They likes it there."

This abundance of natural beauty was an overriding reason people wanted to live in the Grove. But, sometimes, recognition of the area's special qualities seemed to go even further—perhaps a little *too* far. One resident served Key lime pie instead of wedding cake at her daughter's wedding, and the bridesmaids were dressed in Seminole motif. Another Grovite liked to celebrate her birthday each year with a picnic in the Everglades, the birthday cake sporting a large alligator of marzipan with green icing—an endangered species of a different sort.

Outsiders often shook their heads at this attitude of indifference to the conventional. Those who lived there, though, would not live anywhere else in Miami. If it was good enough for Dr. Fairchild and Marjory Stoneman Douglas, it was certainly the place to be. When we first moved to Ingraham Highway and Sunshine Road in 1950, new neighbors reminded us of the old bromide "You don't have to be crazy to live in the Grove, but it helps." They were right.

Alligator cake.

Our modest little neighborhood, two blocks from the bay and a full seventeen feet above sea level, rested on the coral rock rise that runs all the way to Cutler Ridge. It was said to be the trail of the Barefoot Mailman, that well-known figure of South Florida's history who traipsed the shorelines on foot, rain or shine—three days south, three days north—bringing mail to a then sparsely settled region. The fertile land our house was built on had once been part of an early pineapple plantation, a good crop in the days before Hawaii's fertile fields became more accessible. That fabled, rich soil was still there, and everything on our property seemed to sprout almost before it touched the ground (although the astounding growth of our oak trees, we discovered, was not because the land had been cleared to build, giving them breathing room, but because their roots had tapped into the septic tank).

Not far from there was the original Biscayne Bay Yacht Club clubhouse, an old wood-shingle, two-story structure on Hardie Road. Built in 1909, its architect, Walter de Garmo, went on to design the present clubhouse on South Bayshore Drive next door to the Coral Reef Yacht Club. The original is not near the water, which is curious, and sits right across the street from a house built later for Worth Gruelle, son of the author Johnny Gruelle, creator of the beloved Raggedy Ann and Andy books. The property of the de Garmo family, longtime residents of the Grove, is today the site of De Garmo Estates on Douglas Road. Their original homestead once stretched as far south as Cocoplum Circle. Today the compound totals just three acres.

Around the corner from us, on Lennox Drive, was the small house of Dr. Virgil Barker, head of the History of Art Department of the University of Miami and author of several books on his subject. A spry, little, gray-haired man with a goatee and twinkling eye, he once attended an art exhibit where he had served as judge sporting a bright red cocktail napkin in his breast pocket. "To hide the blood," he explained. Anyone who has juried a local show will know to what lengths rejected artists are capable of going. At the cocktail hour (strictly observed in many Grove houses), classical music from his phonograph could be heard emanating from his charming. little wooden abode surrounded by its tall trees.

On Park Avenue, Robert Law Weed, an architect associated with the 1933 Chicago World's Fair, lived in the most traditional of cottages, in contrast to the innovative homes he was creating for his clients. His modern, luxurious, and ingenious designs can still be found throughout the area, but "home is where the heart is," they say.

In that three- or four-block area lived people with an amazing assortment of interests: an ex-banker, the Norwegian parents of the artist John Klinkenberg, a book illustrator, a metal sculptor who had done the artistic lighting and sculptures for the Americana Hotel on Miami Beach (now demolished), a church organist, an ex-mayor of Perrine, a *Herald* columnist, a professor of French, and, my personal favorite, the niece of Isadora Duncan.

Marjory Stoneman Douglas, former journalist and author of *Everglades: River of Grass*, the book that made people understand the importance of our giant aquifer, was just around the corner on Stewart Avenue. Sometimes called the Mother of the Everglades, she lived in a fairy-tale cottage like Hansel and Gretel's, where she resided until her death at the age of 108. The Hugh Matheson property nearby was where the first Hayden mango was developed. The daughter of Mrs. Foster, who lived east of us in those days in the house on the corner of Matheson and Douglas, was Nell Foster Montgomery Jennings, widow of Colonel Montgomery, remembered by the Montgomery Palm Collection at Fairchild Gardens, which he founded, and herself the originator of the "Ramble," which raises funds for the Garden to this day. All of these special people were simply our neighbors.

Whether it was old Dan, our faithful, rain-or-shine Bahamian yardman (who was also a preacher), bicycling every week from Perrine to our house with his hand mower on the handlebars, or José Ferrer, the well-known Oscar-win-

ning actor (for *Cyrano*) and director, who lived across the
street and, indifferent to the onrush of traffic, managed to
wash his car in his front drive on Ingraham Highway, everyone had his space. The Grove's credo of "live and let live"
allowed Sepi Dybronyi, the sculptor of a likeness of Anita
Ekburg (of *La Dolce Vita* fame) to lend his studio in Ye Little
Wood for the filming of *Deep Throat*, and the South
American drug lord on Douglas Road to put a zoo of wild
animals in his back acre, until the noise of the macaws and
the jaguar roaring at night became too much, even for
notably tolerant Grove neighbors.

When new houses continued to be built as far south as
Snapper Creek Lakes and Hammock Oaks, the road traffic
increased until Ingraham Highway sometimes looked like a
parking lot. I often asked my friends, "Why don't you use Le
Jeune Road or US One? It's quicker." "But this is so *restful*,"
they'd reply. "We *love* to drive through the green arcades and
past high hedges after a hard day at the office!"

Over time, however, car emissions began to affect the
soft leafiness of the roadsides, the very attractions that lured
people to the Grove, and today's verdant avenues are much
less shaded and fulsome than they used to be. The constant
fumes and constriction of tree roots have slowly but surely
taken their toll on that high canopy of deep green formed by
banyans (native to India) as relentless traffic snakes its way
south. Today's visitors can only imagine how it used to be.

10

Ear to the Wall

Our Neighbors

The house our neighbor Temple Pearson lived in, on Sunshine Road, had been designed by Marion Manley, architect of the University of Miami's present campus, among many other outstanding projects. It was a perfect little Cape Cod, painted blue with white trim, set among towering oaks on that winding street. It's still there today.

Temple's husband, Philip, a gray-haired man most at ease in, on, or near the water, had been one of the first pupils at the Adirondack-Florida School for Boys, which later became Ransom School and is Ransom Everglades today. With a mere dozen or so boys in the beginning, the first class came from the North in the early 1900s, students whose less than robust health needed the warmth of our winters. The original campus, with its original building preserved, stretches from Main Highway near the village to the bay. Phil Pearson could remember Miami and the Grove from those schooldays. One sight he still loved to recall was the huge, three-masted sailing ships that used to anchor like flocks of birds on Biscayne Bay near the foot of Bayfront Park, bringing timber and other much-needed building supplies to this frontier.

Temple Pearson came from a highly artistic and individualistic family. Her aunt was Isadora Duncan, the colorful and free-spirited innovator of expressive dancing whose end came when her scarf tangled in the wheels of the open car in which she was riding, strangling her to death. Her uncle (and Isadora's brother), Raymond Duncan, an artist with his own studios in Paris, was acclaimed in European circles for his Art Deco designs of textiles and ceramics. His commissions by the very rich to decorate their houses in the early 1920s were highly sought after in those fashionable circles.

A small, brisk, gray-haired woman, Temple loved dogs (almost more than people, I suspected) and came by our house often, walking her own little miniature dachshund and checking unobtrusively on our several pets to be sure we were not neglecting any aspect of their lives. On one of her visits, our conversation turned to travel and she revealed her connections to the Duncan family and the events of a very special trip she had taken when she was a small child. With her mother and cousin, Temple Duncan had accompanied Isadora and the Duncan troupe on a performance tour of Europe. The tour reached Russia in the winter of 1907, when Isadora had been invited to dance privately for the Russian Court at the Winter Palace.

Russia at that time, with its fields of snow and domed churches, must have looked much like pictures in old fairy tales, an amazing experience for an American child. As part of Isadora's entourage, Temple and her little cousin occupied an apartment in the Winter Palace itself, with their governess in charge, while the Duncan dance troupe entertained at a party for the czar's guests. The governess, a German martinet by Temple's account, was a stern and humorless woman whose greatest pleasure was keeping her two little charges under strict control. Even as she remembered her in the telling of the story, Temple shook her head at the very thought of the discipline exacted by the woman.

One evening, as the two children finished their supper and prepared for bed, there was a light knock at the entrance to their rooms. The governess marched forward, opened the door, and fell back in astonishment. Standing there, framed in the light of the hall passage, was a tiny woman swathed in a long, voluminous, white ermine cape and jeweled tiara. It was Anna Pavlova herself, prima ballerina of the famous Russian Ballet! And in her small hands, lavishly covered with sparkling diamonds, she held an enormous box of chocolates. For a moment all speech was lost in the presence of this unexpected visitor.

"These are for the little ones," the diva told the governess, who thanked her obsequiously and promptly took the goodies away to another room, where they might be doled out later for perfect behavior. (A rare occurrence, according to Temple, if the past gave any indication!) The children's eyes longingly followed the disappearing chocolates, and their disappointment could hardly be contained. But no sooner had the governess left the room than Pavlova whispered, "Quick! Hide these!" And from under her snowy cape she produced an identical box of sweets. With a glance in the direction of the absent nurse, she whispered, "I had one just like her! She'll eat them all herself! So these are just for you. Goodnight!" With a smile and a wave of her small, jeweled hand, Pavlova vanished, the box of chocolates disappeared under the bed, and Temple and her cousin secretly feasted on bonbons until the tour ended.

One afternoon, the children were taken to see the playroom of the czar's young son, the Czarevitch Alexi. It was filled with dazzling toys of all kinds, she remembered, amazing playthings culled from the workshops of the best and most inventive toymakers in Europe and the Orient. Among them were a full-size hobbyhorse covered in real pony skin and every imaginable mechanical marvel that could be found to delight the heart of a small prince. Toys filled shelves, cabinets, tables, and floor space in the large room. Though the children were not allowed to touch any of these possessions, just seeing such wonders at a time when toys were few and highly prized was, Temple remembered, an unforgettable experience.

Later, the troupe returned to Paris, where Isadora, then at the height of her popularity and influence, was being fêted and entertained. It was a time of artistic creativity, when modern artists and musicians and ballet masters—the avant-garde of Europe—were producing their most innovative works. Temple, full of the excitement in this charged atmosphere, was allowed to stay up for some of the parties of the life *bohème*, an interesting experience for any youngster, no doubt.

Present at one of these affairs was the great sculptor Rodin, a good friend of Isadora. He was a round, little man with a goatee, Temple recalled, alive with bouncing energy. His sculpture studio was in the same building, and he invited her to see where he worked on the clay models for his largest creations. She remembered a huge, drafty loft with cloth-covered clay studies, armatures on stands, drawings, and numerous works in different stages of progress. Lining the periphery of the rough walls were waist-high cabinets containing dozens of drawers of different sizes and depths. Rodin pulled open some of these to show their contents. As narrow as trays or as large and deep as trunks, they held plaster casts of different parts of the human body in different attitudes, all models to aid the artist. One drawer, for instance, held nothing but ears, another fingers. Others held models of toes or arms or eyes, and all of these were sorted and articulated in every imaginable angle, pose, and aspect the human form might assume. They waited in their dark spaces to express the exact nuance of the great sculptor's concept of his subject. It was a fascinating peek behind the scenes for Temple.

Temple, whose name was derived from that of a popular author of the day, brought a reminder of that bohemian world to the Grove in the person of her uncle Raymond. Founder of his own Art Deco Studios in Greece and Paris, where scarves, murals, and interior design accessories were produced for the haute monde of the 1920s and early 1930s, he was almost as well known on that continent as his famous sister. In a burst of self-expression, he even went so far as to adopt the homespun tunic garb of the ancient Greeks (a culture he greatly admired), a look he wore daily all of his life, complete with headband over straggly gray locks and laced-to-the-knee leather sandals. In this odd regalia, he often visited Temple at her little blue Cape Cod house on Sunshine Road, alighting from his chauffeur-driven limousine looking, some said, like a goatherd. It seemed a natural occurrence in the Old Grove.

Sadly, Temple Pearson knew great disappointment later in life when one of her sons fell in with Murph the Surf, notorious thief of the Star of India gem. In a botched attempt, the jewel thieves tried to rob Olive Wofford, widowed owner of the old Wofford Hotel on Miami Beach and known for her fine jewel collection. The pair tied up Mrs. Wofford and her maid, but in the course of the invasion, the maid managed to free herself and trip the silent alarm. When police arrived, the thieves, caught by surprise, attempted to escape by jumping through a plate-glass window in the Wofford home. Apprehended and jailed, Temple's son later was released from the penitentiary, only to try another jewel caper. He was caught again and returned once more to residency behind bars.

Around the corner from Temple Pearson, our illustrator/artist neighbor, Margaret Schoonover, another animal lover, lived on Matheson in a very old, two-story, wood home on a narrow lot, wrapped in the cool shade of high trees. Its tall, double-hung windows and polished wood floors were the perfect setting for some of the unframed paintings Margaret, who had studied at the Sorbonne, produced in her studio at the back of the property. She and friend Alice Marriott, author of the children's books Margaret illustrated, used to spend the summer months in Santa Fe. There they had built, by themselves, a complete

Southwestern-style home of adobe, where they lived six months of the year. Their biggest problem was transporting back and forth each year the many cats that ruled their household. Since the cats did not like car travel, they spent the tedious trip jumping back and forth and roaming the front seats of the vehicle, desperately seeking a way out of their mobile prison. Two thousand miles of that agitation made the journey an event no one looked forward to.

One year, however, to allay the discomfort of this dreaded excursion, a van was purchased, and the rear interior was totally carpeted to order—floor, ceiling, sides—and a grill was placed between that space and the driver's seat. Carefully, casually, the cats were introduced to their travel arrangements. After a thorough and silent inspection, the "catmobile" was accepted by its intended passengers (grudgingly, to be sure), serenity reigned, and May and November no longer held terror for all concerned. Another case of Grove innovation! Today, a contemporary house has replaced Margaret's secluded studio, and, resourceful to the end, the cats have found other homes.

Alice Marriott, Margaret Schoonover's author/companion, was an ethnologist who was interested in setting down the oral histories and legends of the Southwest Indian culture while the older members of the tribe could still recall them. A graduate of the University of Oklahoma, she had been made a blood sister of the Kiowas, an Oklahoma tribe, during a ceremony she considered a mark of great honor and trust. When the Junior Museum moved to the Miami Woman's Club, Alice was one of those professionals who was generous in contributing time and ideas for its opening exhibit, drawing on her connections at Western museums with Indian collections for loans to the fledgling project. And the result was the arrival of native garb, jewelry, weapons, and masks that ensured the enthusiastic response the show received, clearly demonstrating what Miami might find in its own history.

Gone from the site today, the Miami Woman's Club

used to stand just south of Trinity Church on the bay near the Venetian Causeway, until taxes and falling membership forced its sale to developers. A graceful, three-story building, it offered space to the Junior League–sponsored project in a very central location. Forerunner of the Miami Museum of Science, the Junior Museum, the only museum for children south of Jacksonville at that time, moved from its first cramped site on Biscayne Boulevard and opened its doors with an exhibit mounted on a huge, twelve-foot-high trylon. The show, with its on-loan artifacts borrowed from older, richer museums, traced Indian migration from Asia, over the land bridge that once existed between the continents, running from Siberia along the Pacific Coast and fanning out across the Plains, the Southwest, and then into Georgia and Florida. At each point of the story, the types of homes that the different tribes built, their basketry and beadwork, their masks and weapons were featured on the huge map depicting their migration.

Originally, the Florida panel intended to mark the forts used during the Seminole Wars. (One thinks of Forts Myers, Pierce, Lauderdale, and Dallas.) But research underlined the bloodiness and cruelty of those encounters, and the museum board felt this could be divisive among schoolchildren (some of whom were Native Americans), so only artifacts from the earliest settlements were used.

It was a wonderful show, considering the fact that ingenuity had to carry a large part of the presentation, and it owed much of its success to input from Rand Warren, a new resident formerly with the Museum of Modern Art in New York. His support and guidance were typical of the attitude generously shown by those who had retired here or were just passing through Miami and were happy to contribute to the new project. They loved the area and wanted to offer their special talents. They did so handsomely, and the results convinced local government that it was an idea whose time had come. It is because of the initial efforts of this show's organizers and supporters that the Museum of Science and the Planetarium, now located across from Vizcaya, exist today. And as one of six museums chosen by the Smithsonian to exhibit traveling shows assembled from their attic of extensive collections, and with plans on the drafting board for a new building compound, the Museum of Science is growing and changing with the city. The original house that sheltered the small but ambitious Junior Museum off Biscayne Boulevard, with its simple dioramas and donated artifacts, is fast retreating into memory. Little acorns . . .

Below us, at the foot of Prospect Street, sits a house marked by a high silver dome, barely visible now from the street. Still in place, the dome was once an astronomical observatory, where a large telescope took notice of distant stars in the heavens—before Miami became the city of neon and bright lights it is today, which plays havoc with star-gazing. The house was built by a family from the Great Lakes region, which may account for the addition of another unusual feature—a large yacht basin suitable for ice-breaking. It evidently did not occur to them that ice was a problem seldom encountered in tropical waters. Dr. Carl Henry Davis and his artist wife, Elizabeth, acquired the property in the 1940s, and it was their home for the next fifty years, through hurricanes, floods, and even the discovery of a floating dead body.

One of the hurricanes of the 1960s was an extremely wet one, and there was flooding to a depth of four or five feet in the low-lying area west of the house, extending as far as Douglas Road. Families caught by surprise in one-story homes along Prospect and Battersea put small children on their shoulders and waded through the chest-deep water to Douglas. A flood of that depth will bring all sorts of marine life onshore, some of it even finding its way indoors. And so it was in this storm—baby nurse sharks rode the high water in large numbers, and, stranded by the retreating tide, found themselves swimming over the Davis' kitchen floor. A few even invaded bathtubs, cupboards, and other odd spots. The grandchildren in the family were delighted with the excitement and creatures the storm had brought. After the bad weather had passed and all was calm, they rowed happily around the property in an old rowboat, knowing that in a week or so they would be playing ball on turf that smelled of the sea.

Another storm the Davis house experienced was always remembered by the floating grand piano that circled the living room as the water rose, bumping the ceiling and knocking at walls, its melancholy twanging adding to the cacophony while the storm raged through the night. The Davises marked the storm's progress from the second floor as the piano swirled and crashed, until the water finally receded and the waterlogged and battered instrument sank to the floor. (Furniture was usually moved upstairs when a storm approached, but a piano is another kettle of fish.)

And the dead body? That discovery appeared one afternoon on the occasion of a Davis family birthday celebration for two venerable sisters in their eighties, who were having a drink in the kitchen to toast their numerous years. Outside, a family member sitting on the sea wall noticed a floating object that looked suspiciously like a body bobbing along and called police. In quick succession, several police cars pulled up and the shoreline was soon busy with officers and curious onlookers. A young family member was hurriedly dispatched to the kitchen and charged with keeping the elderly sisters from knowing what was going on in the backyard. Somehow, she managed to keep the two dowagers sipping and chatting, and throughout the ensuing excitement, the octogenarian ladies, unaware of the uninvited guest (a birthday spoiler if ever there was one), merrily toasted each other's longevity, probably thinking they had seen it all in their advanced years!

Elizabeth Davis, an established painter, maintained a separate studio on the property. A great favorite of Grovites, she had many friends who were luminaries of the art world. Her roots were in Chadds Ford, Pennsylvania, which saw her each summer, and her friendship there with painter Andrew Wyeth extended to his talented family.

In the 1960s, the Lowe Gallery was active in introducing Miamians to the International Art movement. Bringing such artists as Dong Kingman, Xavier Gonzalez, Eliot O'Hara, Robert Motherwell, and even Pop Art artist Peter Max to serious students and Sunday painters alike, was a highlight at the Lowe Gallery, named for its original donors, Joe and Emily Lowe (he was known as the Popsicle King). Elizabeth Davis was an important player in convincing many of these artists to come to the cultural desert of Miami, which was just beginning to benefit from traveling shows and community support. The currency they brought afforded an introduction to "happenings," Op Art, and "Happy Accidents." As the new schools emerged, Miami began to learn from the experience, to relax and forget its diffidence in the matters of the art world. It seemed art was not always ART, after all. It was often how verbal one could be in finding meaning in the meaningless. Or, as they used to say, whether you could talk a good game.

Though the Davis home's original five acres have been subdivided and dotted with new houses, the bright silver dome is visible just to the north of that part of the canal where the Coral Gables Waterway spills out into the salt water of Biscayne Bay. The Davises have left, but the echoes linger (and ice has yet to form in that yacht basin).

Still on its site on the bluff above the mouth of the Coral Gables Waterway is a most unusual home built by Charles and Paula Baker—she from a family well known for its Western lumber fortune, he a witty bon vivant and popular writer of cookbooks originally from Orlando. Widely traveled, the Bakers envisioned a home that would incorporate some of the elements they had fallen in love with in the Orient. They were enamored of the beautiful moon doorways found in the Far East and admired the highly glazed peacock-blue roof tiles. They built two large homes on their property twenty years apart, each reflecting some of those elements.

The first house, called Java Head, was subject to the usual rigid building code of Coral Gables in the 1930s. The rules were even less elastic then—even the exterior color was prescribed. (Strong South American architecture, with its wood and stone innovations and bold use of height and line, had yet to invade Cocoplum, which loosened the rules a little later.) Paula characterized the fifty-six hearings, during which the Bakers sought permits for the unique facets of their house, as "nightmares." Nevertheless, in time the beautiful home, with its ballroom, precious-wood finishes, and moon doors, was finally completed, and its vantage point at the mouth of the Coral Gables Waterway offered a magnificent panorama from Key Biscayne south toward the Keys.

It was here at Java Head one evening that Beaux Arts, the volunteer arm of the Lowe Gallery, honored poet Robert Frost, who was wintering at his property in South Miami, called "Pencil Pines." After a succulent buffet, the hundred or so guests found seats wherever they could, including the very top step of the carpeted stairway, to hear the white-haired celebrity. Seated in a large, comfortable armchair (rather like Russell Baker on PBS), he read from his own body of work. The quiet was palpable, the atmosphere mesmeric. Coffee and conversation with the distinguished guest followed, until it became noticeably late for poetry, even where moon doors and a celebrity in one's midst invited it.

When the Bakers built a newer, even more luxurious home, called Java Head East, they took with them an even stronger Oriental feeling in glazed tiles and wood, and the pleasure of quiet, small, green gardens tucked into unexpected places. The home included a ballroom, five sinks for food preparation in the large kitchen, custom-sculpted Chinese rugs, a musicians' gallery, and exquisite wood finishes. The moon-shaped double-door entry to this second house can be seen, if one looks closely, in the James Bond movie *Goldfinger.* Add tennis courts and a dock for their large sailing yacht (the Bakers had a passion for sailing), and this fantasy of its owners, for its owners, and by its owners made for a pleasurable retreat and welcome landfall. In time, the Bakers left Coral Gables for the less crowded shores of Florida's west coast, but Java Head East, now elbowed by The Gables condominiums and others, remains a very special estate.

Drive down Edgewater, a leafy street that makes a steep dip where the underlying coral rock ridge drops off sharply toward the bay, and you will see those luxury condos with their glittering windows and small balconies along the Coral Gables Waterway, their skyward reach effectively blocking the view that used to define the horizon—a view that included Miami Beach, Key Biscayne, and Elliot Key. One has to pay dearly for that view today. With a little neck-straining, you can still glimpse both of the original houses, if the light is right.

Our present style of living may include newer toys, but in many cases, something rather special has been lost. There is not that individual stamp of the owner's taste, which often made homes like the Bakers' so interesting. Instead, a professional is given the last word, and the owner's personality remains elusive. Still, in houses like Java Head and Java Head East, there is a chance that we can know a bit about the original owners, who expressed their choices in evocative ways that make us feel their presence. A backward glance still tells us a little about that time, that place, and those who left their mark.

11

Gates of Paradise

Coconut Grove Estates from the 1920s

The Grove has many estates, and one of the most beautiful in its day was El Jardin (The Garden), now Carrollton School. Before the school buildings presently on the street side of the bayfront property were built, the approach was a lush green façade that framed the wooden double gates set in a low coral rock wall. The vista of the main house remained hidden around the curve of the drive, an anticipatory treat. To the right, just behind the wall at the street side, a charming, little, two-story, coral-rock gatehouse with outside stairs, the happy exuberance of a bright pink coral vine clinging to its rough gray surface, was the only building visible. Eight-foot-high Spanish bayonet plants ran along the approach to the property facing the street and guarded the entrance on either side of the gates, their sharp, dark green spears a warning to all intruders.

Inside the gates, on the left of the winding drive, lay a small garden, square and sunken, surrounded by shady oaks, with sunlight at its center. Down a short flight of lichen-covered stone steps cut into the native rock below lay this cloistered arbor, where a very old brass sundial invited all who passed that way to "Grow Old Along with Me. The Best is Yet To Be." Small flowers filled the crevices of the garden's sunken walls, its air of composure promising a moment or two of serenity and contemplation to any who passed that way.

Up ahead, beyond the leafy curve of the drive, lay the house itself. Wrapped in thick, textured, rose-dappled walls, it was a magnificent example of the Italian palazzo style, designed by the firm of Kiehnel and Elliott in 1917. Its massive hip roof covered in Tuscan red tiles that reflected the sun's warmth, the house was two full stories high, with the added height of an immense, stand-up attic. (When Carrollton first took possession, the attic was full of beautiful Spanish and Italian painted furniture left behind by the previous owners. These pieces found their way into the school's first Christmas antiques sale, a windfall that could never be duplicated.)

Author's sketch of carved pillar at El Jardin.

Heavy, wooden, double entrance doors—painted in soft colors in the Italian manner, studded with brass and wooden bosses, and banded by intricate, scrolled iron hinges and door fittings—centered the front façade. Flanking these were miniature orange trees in stone planters. Across the lintels that topped the wide door and around the twisted pillars on either side, ornate carved leaves and fruits writhed sinuously, inviting one into this Eden. Small casement windows banked either side of the entrance; guarded by thick, ornamental, bronze bars; they lent balance and symmetry to the elegant whole.

Behind these outer doors lay the shadowy foyer, a high-ceilinged, square space with a music room on one side and reception chamber on the other. Cool air, insulated from the tropical heat outside, drifted from the two-story atrium ahead, where rays of pale sunlight filtered down from a large skylight three floors above. The step-down floor of this spacious, square garden room was paved with magnificent oxblood red tiles set in a hexagonal pattern and extending to the steps of a wide, stone staircase at one end. Centered in the quiet retreat, its delicate sprays of water playing in the bars of shifting light, rose a charming, stone fountain of carved cherubs, its pleasant murmuring sounds adding a soothing note to the room.

Romanesque arches surrounded the atrium, their rhythmic pattern emphasizing their classic design as they separated light from shadow at the edge of the loggia. Heavy, six-foot tall, Venetian torchères stood in the half-light of these loggias, their fanciful bases fashioned from large, carved tortoiseshells that carried aloft the twisted, black wrought-iron candelabra.

To the east of the gallery, through French doors, lay an imposing reception room of grand dimensions, a salon that took full advantage of the panorama of Biscayne Bay. It spanned almost the entire width of this Medici-like palace. Massive bronze and glass grilles looked toward the sweep of green lawn that reached to the water's edge—a breathtaking

Luncheon group on the terrace that overlooks the pool at El Jardin in the 1930s.

site that invited the challenges of any formal event. Location, location, location! In this room, an impressive stone fireplace filled the south wall. Overhead, hand-painted wooden beams in gold and soft, rich colors rested under the high ceilings and complemented tapestry-covered Italianate furniture. For all its magnificence, however, this house felt very much like a home—a gracious, if rather grand, one.

A wide balcony terrace with heavy limestone balustrades ran the length of the first floor on the bay side. Twenty feet below lay a wonderful, Olympic-sized pool, deep enough for high dives and lighted at night by the glow of Italian-styled stone lanterns along its copings. Unseen from above was the echoing tunnel that lay under the house (Vizcaya also had one). It emerged at pool level and provided shower facilities and changing rooms for swimmers. This long, twisting black tunnel was dimly lit and had light switches at each end. A favorite prank of Carrollton students in later years was waiting until one of their classmates was halfway into the lighted tunnel, then flipping the switch. Not surprisingly, the sudden darkness produced fierce howls of protest on the part of the now disoriented classmate caught in the echoing abyss, and much glee on the part of the pranksters!

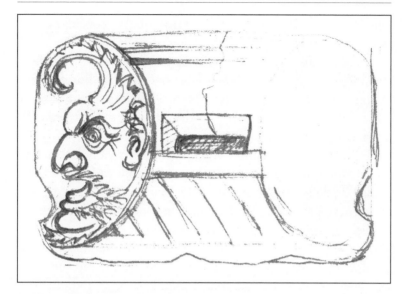

Author's sketch of gargoyle mailbox at El Jardin.

Two curved, stone stairways at either end of the terrace descended to patios with tables and umbrellas, where one could sun or take refreshment, then continued downward to poolside and the bay.

Amusing conveniences underscored estate life at that time. There was, for instance, a smooth marble plaque in the Venetian style high on the wall of the gallery, featuring a pair of grinning gargoyle faces flanking a wide slot, into which guests could drop outgoing mail. Small children were told not to put their fingers near the slot, lest they be nipped by another unseen monster behind the opening. (Letters dropped into a box in the kitchen and from there would be taken to the post office by the next person going into the village.) An old-fashioned gasoline pump with a milky, glass top shaped like a lollipop stood in front of the garage until Carrollton took occupancy. At the time El Jardin was built, no gas stations were open on Sundays, so one needed to plan ahead.

At the farthest end of the property, hidden behind a dense grove of trees, was a large private yacht basin, inviting one to add the water world and its amusements to those of the house. Today, of course, environmental considerations would certainly forbid the dredging of such an amenity.

This beautiful estate, built originally for John Bindley, president of Pittsburgh Steel, later became the home of W. Alton Jones and his family. The local perception was that Jones had at one time been the chauffeur of Henry L. Doherty, founder of Cities Service Corporation and Mr. Jones' mentor. The mantle of president eventually fell on Mr. Jones' shoulders. You can't get much more self-made than that. His daughters attended Miss Harris' School, and their swimming parties with fried chicken luncheons under those umbrellas on the patio terraces, once a must, are probably not as frequent at Carrollton today. But the magnificent pool, with its stone lantern lights for night dips, and the marble masks that guard the mail are still there, testament to a way of life once found behind the private hedgerows of Coconut Grove (and still to be found in smaller versions).

Sadly, though, the little sunken garden has been filled in and paved over. An extra parking lot has been added, but something special has been taken away.

As you pass the coral rock wall with electronic gates at 3551 Main Highway, north of Ransom School, you can see the naturally landscaped grounds of what was at one time the Field estate. Its seven bayfront acres comprised a wedge of land roughly two hundred by fifteen hundred feet, complete with a freshwater spring and several acres of white and red mangroves flourishing on its bayfront. At its center was a two-story Spanish Colonial house of exceptional charm, with arched French doors throughout the downstairs, a beautiful limestone staircase, a built-in safe off the kitchen for silver and valuables, an open pool surrounded by bougainvillea, and a grand sweep of lawn to the bay shore, with a small boat channel bordering the north side. In addition, there was a charmingly simple three-room guesthouse, the likes of which you might find in the jungles of Colombia, with its white walls, screens all around, and a wide porch overhang on three sides. A ruin of a once-charming teahouse and a three-car garage with a servants' apartment overhead completed the compound. The main house, it is said by Grovites, was built with reinforced steel beneath its concrete, water-side façade and survived many hurricanes, including the 1926 killer storm. Surround all of this with more than two hundred different species of trees, some quite rare and monstrously large because of their age, many flowering, with epiphytes and bromeliads thick among their branches, and there it was—Casa Blanca.

For many decades, Casa Blanca was the homestead of Dr. Henry Field and his wife, Julia Allen Field, a woman of delicate beauty, quiet determination, and many accomplishments. Dr. Field, an anthropologist and a graduate of Oxford, specialized in archaeological digs around the Middle East. As part of the Marshall Field clan from Chicago, he moved within an elite circle of world-class artists and scientists that included Buckminster Fuller, of geodesic dome fame; the Leakeys, discoverers of the earliest remains of man; Julian Huxley and C. P. Snow at Oxford; sculptor Henry Moore; and J. R. R. Tolkien, author of *The Hobbit*, to name a very few. Dr. Field himself was the author of several books on anthropology and many papers in his area of research, the mark of a man whose contacts and correspondence reached across the world.

Residence of the Henry Field family in Coconut Grove.

Dr. Field's mother had divorced his father and taken the boy to live with her in England, where she had remarried. She bought the property in the 1940s as a winter home and, it was said, kept an alligator in the bathtub when in residence. One startled visitor reported bestial roars coming from the sun porch on one occasion. Investigation revealed a jaguar in a none-too-sturdy cage, pacing impatiently as he awaited shipment back to the Amazon rainforest. The visitor hastily withdrew.

Although the house saw many distinguished guests and its family was an integral part of the Grove intelligentsia, the most amusing story connected with the house took place after the family had moved on. The beautiful estate was loaned for a month to a group of attorneys from Texas who were in Miami for a very important trial and needed accommodations that would allow them to meet and brainstorm after hours. Their first indication that this was no ordinary house came when they asked for the keys to move in and were told there were none. In the course of updating the property, the heavy wooden front door of earlier times, a bastion of security, had been replaced. The entrance now was an imposing barrier of thick glass—with no lock fittings whatsoever. The object of this new design was to allow approaching visitors to see straight through the house to the other side, where a wondrous view of the bay could be glimpsed through heavy mangroves clustered at the end of the sloping green lawn. Stunning? Yes. Safe? No.

Unusual though this lack of hardware was, the beauty of the setting and its convenience to downtown Miami, plus the security of electronic entrance gates at the front of the property, allayed any misgivings these professionals might have had. So they moved in, enjoying the pool in its setting of purple bougainvillea above the antique stone benches and jardinières; the delights of the trendy Grove; and the luxury of being together in the evening to review their arguments and plan for the following day. That is, until small but valuable items began to disappear. Money, a wallet, a little jewelry was misplaced or lost. After several incidents, members of the group, who did not know each other all that well, suddenly began to wonder about their housemates.

The mystery ended abruptly late one night when one of the attorneys went down to the kitchen for a midnight snack. He was startled to find a strange man—scrawny, unshaven, barefoot, in ragged shorts and pullover—sitting at the kitchen table, strewn with jars and cartons, and eating a peanut butter sandwich.

The two men stared at each other for a moment, each assessing the situation, and then chaos erupted, the interloper frantically dashing through the house, the shouts of his pursuer sounding the alarm and waking everyone else in the house. The man fled up the front stone staircase two steps at a time, down the hall, and finally into the master bedroom, artfully dodging the half-asleep occupants, who by now were milling about in confusion, unable to take in what was transpiring.

Then, in a desperate attempt to elude his pursuers, who now had him cornered, the stranger crashed through the fastened French doors to the balcony, punching out the screens and stripping the doors off their hinges on his way out. Straight into the lighted pool some twelve feet below he dove. It was the stuff of a Douglas Fairbanks movie. A few quick strokes to the end of the pool, and the unwelcome man simply vanished down the lawn toward the bay and the dark of the mangroves.

Police were called, of course, but could not penetrate the swampy mangroves at that time of night and found no trace of the intruder. A half-eaten peanut butter sandwich and broken French doors were the only evidence from the crime scene. It was later surmised the invader must have been a homeless person, sleeping by day and coming out at night from the thick tangled undergrowth at the edge of the bay to raid the refrigerator and steal whatever money or jewelry he could find in the house.

The Texas attorneys, to no one's surprise, left the house the very next day, feeling the Grove had certainly lived up to its reputation as a place where odd things happened but convinced *they* had seen enough to last them for the duration of their visit. I was told, though, they dined out well and frequently, for the remainder of their stay (in a hotel), on the story of Mangrove Man and the house with no keys.

Unfortunately, the sight of police everywhere during the excitement made the landlord's Japanese butler uncomfortable. It seems he had neglected to get a green card when he came to this country from Peru, so he and his wife disappeared overnight. From a full house to a flush in one incident!

At the very end of shaded St. Gaudens Road, a lane that meanders toward the bay side and is lined with some of the oldest homes in the Grove, is the estate built by Willis duPont on six bayfront acres of impeccable green lawn. Mr. duPont went as far as digging a deep-water channel out to the main boat channel in the bay (impossible today), and made plans for a helicopter pad (an annoying and noisy prospect for neighbors). Television cameras were embedded in the entry gates, and all other manner of security was installed. Having done all that, Mr. duPont brought his wife and children to the Grove, intending to stay awhile. But after a spectacular robbery during which his priceless collection of unique and precious antique gold coins disappeared, Mr. duPont thought it over and moved his family to Palm Beach.

The lavish residence was then sold to an Arab prince. The estate's enormous boathouse, vast and echoing and adequate to house a very large yacht, was almost larger than the mansion it served and was a marvel of engineering, boasting a magnificent, vaulted ceiling of arched and polished wooden beams soaring two stories high. Each giant support had been meticulously pressure-curved by European craftsmen to conform to its counterpart through an exacting heat process—an impressive display of artistic carpentry.

Under the sheik's ownership, the house was seldom occupied except for servants and a custodian. Sometimes a year or two would go by without a visit from him, but the house was always kept ready for his arrival whenever the caprice might seize him. Indeed, this particular home was only one of a great number that he owned in different parts of the world, many much larger and all designed to accommodate his extensive entourage. In this Grove estate, it was said, the countless bedrooms of the main house were refurbished every two years by New York decorators, who replaced carpet and furnishings whether the rooms had been occupied or not. A Coconut Grove legend? Who knows?

The sheik's brother-in-law (not royal, just married royal) considered residency in the Grove himself and showed interest in a property not far distant, on the water. One summer afternoon, he and his retinue arrived at the appointed hour in his armored, fire engine–red Rolls Royce. His bodyguards immediately leaped out, with walkie-talkies squawking, and demanded that the owners' several pet dogs, who had begun barking and running around the car, be confined before the potential buyer would get out of the vehicle. Arrangements were hurriedly improvised, and the dogs whistled to their kennel.

On being shown into the house, with its carved portico and lotus-shaped fish pool with water lilies at the entrance, the distinguished viewer immediately asked which way was east. The agent, pointing to the impressive bayfront panorama and anticipating approval of the view, smilingly assured him that that was east. At this information, the entire party upended themselves as they fell on their knees in prayer.

That brief duty done, an inspection of the premises began. Just the male members of the group accompanied the sheik's brother-in-law on a tour of the seven-acre property. Left outside were his two wives and a couple of well-mannered small children. A striding walk to the bay, much rapid conversation in Arabic, male hands gesturing emphatically, and the visit was abruptly over. The walkie-talkies squawked again, the red Rolls roared away, and the dogs were let out to run down the drive, barking goodbye.

It was later announced in local papers that this person had chosen to buy on prestigious Star Island, bastion of wealth and privacy. There he annoyed his affluent neighbors with outlandish additions to his property (a clock tower was one affront), arguments with his contractors that ended up in the courts, and, eventually, sudden flight to the Middle East when bankruptcy reared its ugly head, leaving his creditors to pick through the unfinished construction for salvage. Restitution was not forthcoming from his wealthy in-laws. After all, there *are* limits to what a sheik will do for his sister's husband. Luckily, the Grove escaped having its limits tested as well.

12

Echo Chambers

Bayview Road, St. Gaudens Road

L apped by the shallow waters of the bay at the end of St Gaudens Road sits a house that has been handsomely added to, enhanced, and modernized, but was once the center of an unsolved mystery in the village's early days. Located directly across from the duPont estate, the original dwelling, built in 1914, was the home of a man and his daughter, who lived there quietly, part of the little neighborhood that lay down that shaded lane.

One certain evening, the young woman attended a social event in the company of a young man of her acquaintance, returning home around midnight. Those facts can be substantiated. In the early hours of the morning, however, neighbors awoke to find the house engulfed in flames. The fierce blaze consumed almost all of the structure before help could arrive, trapping the young woman and her father in the roaring inferno. It was not clear why they had not tried to escape or cried out in alarm. Puzzling questions immediately arose. How had the fire started? Had the father and daughter suffocated, perhaps, before the fire was discovered?

Or had they been murdered, the fire then set to cover the fact? Did the young man play a part in this possible crime? Rumors flew and the newspapers sensationalized the mystery. But satisfactory answers were never found.

In time, the house was rebuilt on that site, where charred ruins once traced its foundation, and though its murky and unsettling story might give some nervous souls pause, its coral rock wall and green lawns conceal any hint of its disastrous history. Whatever secrets it hides of that night long ago, St. Gaudens Road remains silent. And any ghosts have long departed.

To the south of the sheik's estate, off the circle of Bayview Road on the bay, is the former home of Alice Wainwright, attorney-at-law and one-time Miami city commissioner. A small, energetic, no-nonsense figure, she was kindness itself toward those who were most vulnerable. Nevertheless, she invariably told you what she thought. You always knew where you stood with Alice.

At the age of thirty-eight and newly widowed, with a young son and her own mother to care for, she earned her law degree from the University of Miami. Hewing to her staunch New England values, Alice established her law practice and proceeded to contribute in numerous ways to the community she had chosen. A great believer in serving her community, she presided as president of the Audubon Society for a term, was an active member of Fairchild Tropical Gardens and a friend to other nature conservancy groups, and held a place on the committee for the Tri-Rail project, which brought rapid transit plans to Miami. Alice was an irreplaceable asset to the Grove she loved. Her lifetime of public service and involvement are remembered today in the park on Brickell Avenue named for her.

Her house at the end of the cul-de-sac, a gray two-story built in 1924, was not remarkable in design. But it was pleasant, open to the bay breeze, and in a setting that featured rare plantings and at least one tree species bearing her name. Alice spent her winters there with her adored and spoiled

English springer spaniel, Nicky (what other dog would be flown to Boston for an eye exam?), and her ancient but recognizable-throughout-the-village Mercedes-Benz. Just off the circular drive at her front door was a separate entrance for her law office. There, over the years, she represented a true cross-section of the Old Grove, from Bahamian gardeners to many of the first families in the area, including the Grosvenor family of *National Geographic* ownership. In the course of her practice, she broke new ground. When the Grosvenor estate on Douglas Road, Hissar, was to be replatted as a compound for family members, it was Alice who established the original rules for a Planned Use Development (PUD), the first recorded in Miami.

Alice's late husband's distinguished family connections included Robert Livingston, the eighteenth-century American whose service to his country in the time of President Thomas Jefferson included his appointment as Minister to France. In the corner china cabinet of Alice's dining room was the beautiful porcelain tea set presented by the French government to Livingston in appreciation of his friendship and service in the matter of the Louisiana Purchase. These delicate treasures, executed in a creamy, soft-paste Limoges porcelain and hand-painted in heavy 18-kt. gold, were part of the specially commissioned set of cups, saucers, and serving pieces made for the Minister. The complete dinner service, Alice said, was packed in barrels in a warehouse in Washington, D.C., waiting perhaps to be given to some historical museum. It was fascinating to see this valuable bit of commemorative history and to consider where it had been, within what illustrious context it had been assembled, and how very far it had come to its resting place in the dark corner of the dining room of an old house in Coconut Grove by Biscayne Bay.

One day, as we discussed the coming hurricane season and Nicky rolled on the little Aubusson carpet at our feet, Alice pointed to a large, curious area of mismatched wood on the hardwood floor of the living room in front of the fireplace. She recalled that the '26 hurricane had so flooded the house that the owner, in desperation, had chopped a large hole in the floor to let some of the bay water out. Afterward, the spot had been patched, but the repair was still visible, forever a reminder of that storm and that story.

The site of Alice's property, a five-acre piece with a high rise from the water's edge, included, like many along the bay shore in the Grove, an acre and a half along the shoreline, which was thickly bordered by mangroves crowding a small patch of beach. As with all such property, this undeveloped land, as well as any submerged land included in the legal title, was taxed by the city. Originally, the value in owning such coastal frontage and submerged land was protection of the property it abutted. This allowed for future use (docks, jetties, etc.), thus adding greatly to the property's value. In fact, such title often carried with it riparian rights dedicated to bay access for dry-land neighbors on the same street.

In the 1980s, environmentalists suddenly realized the part mangroves play in our ecosystem, and noted the rate at which they were being decimated, which led to the enact-

Author painting the mangroves in watercolor. Lots of clean water to work with.

ment of strict government rules concerning these plants. In the beginning, they could be cut to the height of five feet. Then the rules permitted just the white mangroves to be disturbed, not the red. Finally, it was adjudged that no mangroves could be cut. At the same time, owners continued to pay taxes on this land even though nothing could be done with it. To many, it seemed like confiscation, and some people brought suits on this point of law, charging that the government had "taken" their property through governmental regulation instead of through eminent domain, thus depriving them of compensation for the loss. This later became a bone of contention regarding "wetlands" in other parts of the country. But the new federal rules were strict and unbending, and to make sure no mangroves were being disturbed, observer planes frequently photographed the shoreline, establishing a microfilm library for future comparison.

Alice was so respectful of nature that she had never touched this feature of her property, but when she finally put her house on the market, finding it too large for her advancing years and failing health, potential buyers could not see the advantage of waterfront prices for land whose waterfront could not be used. So while others had built sea walls and yacht basins before moratoriums became a fact of life and now enjoyed their property fully, Alice's property bore heavy restrictions with severe fines and penalties for noncompliance. (This was before mitigation became an option—agreeing to plant mangroves in a new location in exchange for destruction of some existing—a plan that enabled some developers to build later on.) In any case, her house was taken off the market and Alice Wainwright remained there until her death. Her abiding consolation was that her neighbors, of whom she was very fond, would not have the specter of possible development to worry about.

One July day, when she was summering at her house in Maine, Alice phoned and asked me to go to her office and retrieve some legal papers for her, as I had been left with keys. The neat little office that adjoined the house was cool

13

Ever-Ever Land

Attractions and Amusements

Miami in the 1930s was a hothouse of tourist attractions inspired by the unique natural elements of the area. Such curiosities were worth the sometimes-arduous side trips required to find them. Among the most popular were Parrot Jungle, where trained macaws performed tricks; Monkey Jungle, where visitors were caged and the monkeys ran free; Orchid Jungle; and the Serpentarium, with its twenty-foot-high plaster cobra out front, where visitors could watch cobras being milked for their venom.

And, of course, there were the wonderful pool shows at the Biltmore Hotel, where Johnny Weismuller gave swimming lessons for a time and the loose-limbed Ray Bolger (the Scarecrow in *The Wizard of Oz)* entertained. Here, on Sunday afternoons before World War II, aquacades featuring water ballet and diving clowns preceded the grand climax at the end of the afternoon, when a thrashing alligator was thrown into the deep end of the "largest pool in America" for a wrestling demonstration. The offer of a free swim was

Sunday pool show at the Biltmore Hotel. The orchestra played from a raft in the center of the deep end.

made to the spectators. No volunteers ever spoke up.

On the banks of the Miami River around NW 25th Avenue was the Musa Isle Seminole Indian Village, where women from the Miccosukee tribe worked hand-cranked sewing machines as they sat on the bare plank floors of their elevated chickee huts, stitching the intricate designs of their native shirts, with their full-shaped long sleeves, and the wide, flowing skirts that swept the ground as they walked (always barefoot). Their necks, chests, and ankles were laden with ropes of colored beads Their shiny black hair was combed smoothly in straight strands over large fan shapes, some eight or ten inches high.

The men of the village served as knowledgeable guides to hunters and fishermen. They ventured confidently into the heart of the Everglades in their flat-bottom boats, poling through thick swamp grasses in water that was sometimes barely inches deep. No landmarks that the untrained eye could discern marked that level and shimmering world, only a few sparsely scattered hummocks where birds or small deer might rest. It was a strange water land, but one in which the Seminole could survive. A foray into that endless terrain, where one could easily be lost for days without expert direction, was rewarded, inevitably, by the sight of the shifting

Seminole child dressed like her mother.

beauty, that mixture of solid and liquid, and the tropical bird and animal life found nowhere else in the United States.

By far, however, the greatest attraction for the average tourist was the mesmerizing spectacle of alligator wrestling. In the village compound lay a deep mud pit the size of a small room, surrounded by boardwalks and railings, a raised platform jutting up out of it. The holding pen contained gators of different sizes and stages of wakefulness, some bearing deep scars or missing a limb lost in battle with a cantankerous neighbor. With eyes unblinking they lay, silent as the bumpy green-gray logs they resembled, hissing a menacing warning through slowly widening jaws when jostled by another in the pit.

From this deceptively torpid mass the Seminole wrestler selected an opponent and hauled it up onto the platform by its tail. Then, with a lightening motion, the massive jaws with overlapping teeth were first clamped tightly shut and then held firmly by the wrestler, now astride the creature's back. Avoiding that heavy, lashing tail, a weapon that could easily kill a man, the protagonist, resplendent in his Seminole shirt, in one quick move flipped the gator on its back with a resounding thump, rendering it almost helpless. Then, by repeatedly stroking the reptile's scaly white belly, the wrestler quickly put it into a hypnotic sleep that usually lasted several minutes. As the applause subsided, the alligator was rolled over and pushed back into the mud below, landing on its fellow captives with much grunting and snapping as it slithered off into the mud.

Close observation of the wrestler's hand sometimes revealed a missing finger or two from past performances that had a very different ending. Win some, lose some.

For a short time, Miami also had, by default, a downtown aquarium, which made its home in a large sailing ship. In 1929, the barkentine had been destined to be converted to a hotel, but in transit to its new berth it had, unfortunately, foundered in the channel used by large vessels to reach the Port of Miami. Reduced to a tangled wreck of rigging and broken fragments, it was finally maneuvered to the northern edge of Bayfront Park, a stone's throw from Flagler Street and the Biscayne Boulevard hotels, where it lay, rotting and derelict, a blight on the park's view of fishing piers with their boats, multitudes of greedy pigeons, and, at the south end, close to the mouth of the Miami River, the little white band shell where Cesar La Monica gave concerts under the stars. Since the Depression had put low-priority projects on hold and no money could be found to tow the vessel out to sea or repair it, it was some years before a solution to convert the eyesore into something useful could be found. That solution was a tourist attraction: an aquarium.

Such an exhibit was simpler then than it would be today. In those days, most visitors to an aquarium would expect a glorified fish tank—and that's what they got. The darkened hold of the ship's huge white hulk was fitted with enormous, thick-glass aquarium tanks, lights, pumps, and fans. Until its exhibits died or lost their attraction, it served to display huge sea turtles, a shark or two, and a variety of small tropical fish, crabs, and other ocean life trapped in the murky green water, a dim undersea world that vibrated from the constant throb of pumps filtering salt water from the bay that surrounded it.

Exotic and colorful personalities seemed to drift to the Miami area, capturing the amused attention of visitors and underlining the mosaic that Miami had become. "Silver Dollar Jake," a well-known local character famous for his impulsive distribution of those coins, drove the boulevards in a red El Dorado convertible, the top down, his pet red macaw preening long tail feathers as he clung to the radio antenna.

No less a subject of curiosity was Colonel Green, the son of Hetty Green, known as "the witch of Wall Street," a miserly millionaire octogenarian (the stingiest, according to the *Guinness Book of World Records*), who put pockets for cash and bonds under the long black skirts she always wore. He, in contrast, bought a diamond collar for his pet lap dog.

And swinging from the limbs of trees near Simpson Park every day was the Tarzan Lady, a septuagenarian in a leotard, doing her daily calisthenics among the leaves.

In an era when Ripley's "Believe It or Not" was a hugely popular newspaper feature showcasing oddities of all kinds (Ripley himself once moored his red Chinese junk at a pier in Bayfront Park), the tropics provided their own kinds of curiosities made from native flora and fauna. In the windows of Flagler Street shops in the early 1930s, one could see small stuffed alligators, jaws agape, mounted in various attitudes, a light bulb in their gullets. Heavy alligator handbags were clasped shut with huge saurian claws, sharp nails and all. Necklaces were fashioned from coconut pearls, sea beans, shells, and rosary peas (until it was discovered these last were poisonous). And everywhere one saw dried coconuts simulating mummified human heads, withered and dark brown, wearing startling eyes and teeth of white shells and painted with fierce expressions. Thankfully, that macabre display has vanished, but it would not surprise me to learn that a few of these grotesqueries still lurk in some dark attic in Milwaukee or Oklahoma today, the forgotten souvenirs of an early tourist's trip to Miami.

Even the simple activity of watching the graceful Pan Am flying boats touch down at Dinner Key could provide a novel attraction on drowsy Sunday afternoons. At first, one could see only a far-off speck in the sky, a dot that soon became the plane as it approached, then glided to a gentle landing several hundred yards from shore. Feathering its propellers and cutting the motors, the clipper ship swung around and taxied to the dock, trailing a froth of dancing whitecaps in its wake. There, passengers (eight or ten on the smaller planes) disembarked to go through customs. Uniformed stewardesses (Pan Am was the first airline to have cabin attendants), dressed in navy blue with gold braid, saw them into the terminal.

Arrival safely completed, the aircraft taxied within a few yards of shore, where the water was chest-deep. Two or three airline mechanics in bathing suits then swam out to the plane to attach chains and secure huge, balloon tires under the pontoons, a prerequisite to hauling the craft up a wide concrete ramp on to dry land and into one of the two huge hangars to the north of the terminal for repairs and

A graceful Pan Am flying boat at the Dinner Key Terminal.

MIAMI TERMINAL OF PAN-AMERICAN AIRWAYS. FLA.   A96

Pan Am terminal and hangars at Dinner Key. Once a World War I naval base, the terminal is now the City of Miami City Hall.

storage. Those metal hangars later became dry-dock space for the Merrill-Stevens Boatyard, and still later a boxing gym used on occasion by Cassius Clay (as Muhammad Ali was then known). Their gaunt frames are still there today, neighbors of Monty Trainer's and Chart House Restaurants, surrounded by crowded parking lots.

That Pan Am terminal, once the banner of an airline that accessed ports around the world and that in 1935 made Miami the largest airport of entry in the United States, is today Miami City Hall. What started life as a U.S. naval base in World War I is still the centerpiece of that portion of Coconut Grove on the bay. In its vast, stylish, white Art Deco lobby, with its double vaulted ceiling and mezzanine railed with chrome, once sat a large revolving globe—amazing in its time—that traced vividly all the overseas routes of the airline. The globe was positioned slightly below floor level, its deep pit surrounded by a guardrail so one could lean over and watch as the world moved around slowly.

Years later, when the building was refurbished as City

THIS GLOBE OF THE EARTH –

Is steel; weight 3¾ tons; diameter 10 feet; circumference 31 feet, 5 inches

Shows airlines of the world, in addition to chief geographical features, including ocean depths.

The globe is oriented so that its axis parallels the axis of the earth underfoot. Its North Pole pointing to the North Star.

On this scale (1 inch to 64 miles) the greatest ocean depth, 34,218 feet just east of the Philippines – would be only ⅒ of an inch below the surface of this ball, showing that, compared with the bulk of the earth, the great oceans are relatively only a thin covering of water.

The deepest man has gone beneath the surface of the earth (William Beebe, who descended 2,200 feet into the ocean at Bermuda) would on this scale be scarcely through the paint – ⅟₆₀ of an inch down.

The highest man has ascended off the earth (Captain Albert W. Stevens, 14 miles) would be but ¼ of an inch off the surface of this globe.

The world's highest mountain (Mt. Everest in the Himalayas, 29,141 feet) would project less than ⅒ of an inch from this globe's surface.

All the people in the world, packed into a box, could on this scale be contained in a case less than ⅟₁₀₀ of an inch each way in size.

PAN AMERICAN
AIRWAYS SYSTEM
MIAMI, FLA.

The globe as it sat in the lobby of the Pan Am terminal. Today it is at the Museum of Science.

Hall, that well-known feature was about to be discarded. Fortuitously, Marianne Reynolds (at one time married to the heir of the Reynolds tobacco fortune) rescued it from destruction and presented it to the Museum of Science, where it sits today. And like the world today, it seems to have shrunk.

In this time of worldwide sports coverage accessed by the flick of a finger on a remote control, it is difficult to recall how prominently attendance at the New Year's Day Orange Bowl game played in the social scene. Every successful businessman or political official had a box or seats near center field; photographers from the local papers roamed the stands; festive parties revolved around the spectacle and its visiting celebrities. Miami's society matrons planned what they would wear many months ahead, and because one was always optimistic that the weather would be cooler in January, their dressmaker suits were often wool with the de rigueur hats, gloves, matching shoes, bags, and, of course, chrysanthemum corsages. However, the temperature was almost invariably in the eighties at game time, leaving many spectators feeling they had partied too late and too well the evening before and regretting the woolen suits, no matter how fashionable.

When the present Orange Bowl stadium was completed (barely) and opened for the first time for the New Year's Day game in 1948, my husband and I and another couple were concerned that there would be a great throng with no place to park, so we decided to go a little early and take a small lunch. The game was to start at 2:00 P.M. At noon we arrived to find a vast concrete bowl, lacking finishing touches and looming larger than anything else in Miami in those days. Not another soul had yet arrived in this empty amphitheatre, whose concentric, backless cement benches rose in gray spirals, shimmering under a hot and cloudless sky.

There was a strong breeze, however. And not unlike a small Saharan sandstorm, it lifted the concrete grit from every cranny of the new construction and spun the tiny missiles in every direction. The resulting whirlwind stung one's legs and eyes mercilessly. Our sandwiches, in turn, collected bits of the flying debris; wax paper wrappers and paper cups took off willy-nilly like kites; jackets and skirts flapped wildly; and it was with relief that we finally saw more spectators arrive. However ignoble the thought, we felt their presence would serve as a buffer for the swirling sand that no one had thought to sweep away. We were only too willing to share, feeling confident there was more than enough for everyone! The early bird sometimes gets more than he bargained for (but we *did* get a good place to park).

Besides its football games, the Orange Bowl in its early days became a popular venue not only for sports events but for other entertainment spectacles. On one occasion, Sonja Henie brought her Ice Show to Miami, and a huge skating rink was built in the Bowl for the evening performances. It was a wondrous sight, in this land that melts the ice in one's drink almost instantly, to see skiers whizzing down tall slides bearing flaming torches in a darkened stadium and skaters spinning effortlessly on real ice!

Like the clouds of pigeons that claimed Bayfront Park,

each winter season saw the arrival of the dark blue and silver trailer of astrologer Professor Seward who set up shop across from what is now the DuPont Plaza Hotel at the mouth of the Miami River. A balding man with glasses, he seemed a small wizard holding secrets unimagined. As he orated through loudspeakers from the window of his vehicle, curious passersby often slowed, then stopped, and a crowd soon gathered, mesmerized by his predictions of their star-driven futures as well as by character readings from their astrological signs, and, not incidentally, an invitation to purchase his books. Some, of course, might have consulted him in the past, with less-than-promised results, and these came back to challenge him the following winter, but he always managed to reinterpret their litany of complaints (using what we would call today "spin") and win them back for another "reading" or still more predictions of an interesting future. With the coming of spring, he closed his trailer, heading for another destination, and conversed with the stars until autumn winds brought him back again.

And so each year one could mark the start of "The Season" by the faithful hucksters who made the trek to this

FISHING FROM COUNTY CAUSEWAY. MIAMI SKYLINE IN DISTANCE, FLORIDA

Fishing for dinner from the causeways was allowed then.

city, where the sun shone all winter, there was easy money to be made, and, if worse came to worst, one could always become a beachcomber. Getting dinner was often as simple as dropping a hook and line off the rail of a causeway (possible only in certain spots today), and it was easy to find mangoes or grapefruit or avocados or guavas on trees that overhung the sidewalks and dropped their fruit to the ground. The biggest attraction of all could well have been the freedom from many of the maintenance chores that burdened people in other parts of the country in the winter months. If, added to these advantages, there were the occasional revival tent meetings (free), the annual circus train (free), and diving and bathing beauty contests (free), it is easy to see there was always something more up ahead. For visitors from small places, it was, indeed, the Magic City.

14

Summer Solace

The Days of Summer

During the Depression, it was the consensus of local leaders that snowbirds left too soon after Easter, thus shortening the important boost in the economy that winter visitors invariably brought. An advertising campaign with the slogan "Stay Thru May!" was devised in the hope they would look past the negatives of summer heat and closed shops and extend their stay. The invitation was splashed on huge billboards, blared on the radio, and touted in newspapers (especially Northern publications). But it was an idea that needed justification.

The poinciana trees that bloomed from May to June became the inducement to keep people here a little later in the year. Like canopies of little red orchids, these trees, alight with their flame-colored blossoms, marked the soft green of late spring and early summer with breathtaking splendor. They lined the parkways of South Miami Avenue (and still enhance our landscape in single stands) with their glory, scattering delicate, bruised petals that left a dark red carpet around their smooth, silver trunks. This display was always short-lived and vanished when the summer rain patterns began. This annual show of nature inspired the Royal Poinciana Festival, a pageant that chose a queen and her court and hosted attendant festivities. The pageant was short-lived and vanished after World War II, but the beauty of the trees retain their ability to stun and can still be found in paintings in almost every amateur art show. The trees, with their crowns of color and graceful spreading shapes, are still bright spots in the verdant green of summer and reward those who stay through May.

In spite of such diligent efforts, there was not very much to keep visitors here beyond June. Before air conditioning, one found many activities too uncomfortable. Out-of-season Miami belonged once again to the local residents. As the temperatures rose, the pace slowed. The town became quiet, almost deserted. Men who worked in downtown offices wore white linen suits and panama hats, or blue-and-white seersucker jackets and trousers and straw boaters, and mopped their faces frequently with large, rumpled white handkerchiefs. In the stuffiest office cubbyholes, a towel was sometimes draped across the back of the neck to ensure the cleanliness of one's paperwork.

Watermelon gardens, outdoor places that served ice-cold melon, sprang up on vacant lots, with little tables or benches and strings of electric lights around their perimeter. Darkened porches, where one listened to crickets and watched lightning bugs, gave off the sound of creaking porch swings. Movie houses cooled by huge fans blowing over big blocks of ice became popular. Miami Beach became comatose, closing up everything but the ocean, which at that time one could access at almost any point for miles along the shore, by side roads that branched off the parallel ocean road and headed east to the golden sand dunes covered with sea grape and sandspurs.

On Lincoln Road, the tonier shops were shuttered tight and their counterparts opened in Newport or on Martha's Vineyard to wait out the summer months. The storage facility on Washington Avenue (the site today of the Wolfson Museum) received its usual plunder of Persian carpets rolled in mothballs, Steinway Baby Grands, packed porcelain, covered oil paintings, and greased silverware (Vaseline kept out the salt air) from the homes of the winter residents, who would send their employees ahead again in November to open their homes for the season and restore those furnishings to their proper places.

A favorite expression in those days was "You could shoot a rifle down Flagler Street and not hit anybody." Anyone who could get away usually went to the Carolinas to cool off, the closest point for a change of weather and a little altitude. The only break in the doldrums of summer might come in the form of a hurricane, bringing the welcome smell of rain on a cool breeze. Everyone had a favorite way of predicting whether a storm would hit that year. Some found clues in what the Seminoles predicted at their annual Green Corn Dance, others in how high the saw grass was that year. These were the extent of warnings and predictions in a time when people depended on a barometer and observations from ships at sea. Since this was marginally better than guessing, that still left plenty of room for surprises. But hurricanes were to be expected in a tropical clime, and one was not averse to a small "blow" clearing the stagnant air, cleaning out overgrown foliage, and providing a little excitement—making autumn seem not so far away.

With no air conditioning, the tropical weather of July and August called for long evening drives in the car, usually down Biscayne Boulevard, with its early hotels—McAllister, Alcazar, Columbus, Everglades—past the string of filling stations that lined the street along today's Bicentennial Park (sometimes called Gasoline Alley); past the huge animated billboards of the little Coppertone girl showing off her tan and Johnny Walker doffing his hat above it all; past the huge Belcher Oil holding tanks at NE 15th Street, and then across the County Causeway to Miami Beach. Then along the ocean, where a broad cement sidewalk ran from the Roney Plaza Hotel to the

Pancoast, marking the soft rhythm of the surf, the smell of salt in the languid breezes off the water, the rattling of palm fronds that could sound like a sudden shower of rain.

Or perhaps a trip north of the city, past the "Chicken Hotel," as it was often referred to. It was a boom-time structure that started out as the Fritz Hotel but was abandoned, half-completed, when the Depression grew deeper, leaving its black steel skeleton dwarfing the buildings around it. An eyesore for years, its vacancy finally ended when hundreds of chickens from an egg farm took possession of two floors. At least they went to bed early, as the old adage has it, for it was always dark when one went by. Then a slow drive out to the area that used to be the Graham Dairy (owned by the family of Senator Bob Graham), now the home of Miami Lakes, where the smell of high, sweet, cool grass, glinting with tiny lightning bugs, hung in the humid air. Cooler and drowsy, one headed back home, too relaxed to complain about singing mosquitoes invading one's bedroom or tossing on too-warm sheets.

Light, loose clothing; cold treats like iced watermelon or sherbet; a swim in the ocean (with an eye out for jellyfish, barracuda, stingrays, and sharks), and staying out of the sun, if possible, was the drill for the hot daytime hours. Or spending a muggy afternoon strolling through the shady arcades of downtown store buildings could be refreshing, for these wind tunnels guaranteed a strong, cool breeze when there was no stir of air anywhere else and vapors of steam rose straight up from the softened asphalt streets and dusty sidewalks. Drugstore cowboys watched idly as matrons clutched unsteady hats and breeze-flipped skirts when passing through these shortcuts, but everyone welcomed any small breather from the midday temperatures.

When it was just too hot to cook, there was always the popular drive-in and tall, frosty ice cream sodas to finish off a meal of chicken-in-a-basket or spicy barbecue. Young carhops, not quite out of high school and dressed in shorts, tops, and little aprons, roller-skated around the parked cars, setting up wide trays of cholesterol, while car radios (in top-down convertibles for the lucky one) broadcast satisfying selections from bands like Tommy Dorsey's or Benny Goodman's swinging out "Marie" or "String of Pearls." Smooth music that renewed the spirit. Cool before cool.

Eventually, the long hot days, one very much like the next, gave way to the less humid, more invigorating sunny clime of the season, and life in Miami moved forward again.

15

You Can Get Here from There

The Junior Museum

On Biscayne Boulevard, just north of the Christian Science Church, a two-story 1920s' house on the northwest corner of NE 26th Street became the birthplace of one of the city's best-known attractions. It's an area that was once home to many successful Miami families, then became a neighborhood that had slowly lost cachet through neglect and decay.

In the late 1940s, the Junior League of Miami was looking for a project to put the dividends of its war bonds into and realized there was an area of museum sponsorship that did not require huge endowments or attics full of fine art. It would be a Junior Museum, a project that would offer a place to give children a modest introduction to cultures in other parts of the world through artifacts, costumes, household utensils, and jewelry, among other things, and to inspire them to visit larger museums in other parts of the country when they traveled. The idea finally became reality in 1949, when the museum's first home was located in the old two-story on Biscayne Boulevard with hardwood floors and a handy, if dilapidated, garage apartment for its new director, Nancy Golden, daughter of the head of the Children's Museum in Indianapolis. A good thing, for her salary would hardly have covered rent. Lots of paint, long hours of work from diligent members, and donated exhibits and expertise launched the venture.

Dioramas and loaned treasures were all the Junior League had to work with initially. Inside the first-floor entry, there was a modest display of live snakes, turtles, and small creatures such as hamsters, a raccoon, and baby gators to liven the experience, which was new to most children. A life-size cutout of a fierce caveman with a club crouched in the shadow of the stair landing. There were Seminole artifacts on loan from the University of Florida, courtesy of Miamian Dr. John Goggin—fine basketry, ankle turtle rattles, and shell tools. On the second floor were cultural exhibits describing the daily life of children in other parts of the globe.

Because this was a fledgling effort, mistakes were certainly made. A Guatemalan costume in a case too close to an unshaded window went back to its owner with a big faded spot on the skirt, and a priceless Audubon print generously given by a donor was scissor-trimmed to fit a handy frame, thus destroying a good part of its value.

Upstairs, a friend of the project had donated a hive of live honeybees, which hung in mid-air outside a locked front window overlooking the Boulevard. Two black bears were painted on the inside wall on either side of the sealed window, a lively pair intent on robbing the hive as the bees made their golden treasure. Through the windowpane, children could watch from the cut-away side of the hive as the drones flew in and out, going about their honey-making activities, totally unaware of inquisitive eyes.

On a certain sunny afternoon, the bees suddenly began swarming as two queens found themselves in residence at the same time. The beekeeper was summoned. In his beekeeper hat, swathed with yards of netting, with his protective goggles in place and thick gloves wrapped around a large smoke bomb, the "bee" man climbed up and precariously straddled the steeply pitched gable roof outside the window. High above the heavy afternoon traffic, the mysterious, shrouded figure, veiled in clouds, netting, and angry insects, moved back and forth, intently going about the business of subduing outraged nature. Sporadically, large white puffs of smoke rose skyward, attracting the attention of drivers in the passing traffic below. It is not recorded how many fender-benders took place as people slowed, honked, and tried to see what was going on above the rooftops. However, in the time it takes to play "Flight of the Bumblebee," man triumphed over the laws of the hive, removing one of the queens and leaving the now-settled bee community to carry on its mission. And on the boulevard, all thoughts of men from outer space subsided.

In three years, the museum became successful enough to move to larger quarters in the Miami Woman's Club building, next door to Trinity Church near the Venetian Causeway. Unexpectedly, during this move, the director met an archaeologist from the University of Florida, married, and left to spend her honeymoon in either a hummock or a hammock in the Everglades (I forget which she said).

Unofficial help for the tiny museum in the interim between directors came from winter visitors Rand Warren, who had been with the Museum of Modern Art in New York, and Alice Marriott, ethnologist, writer of children's books about Native Americans of the Southwest, and my neighbor in the Grove. The project stayed on track.

As is its custom, the Junior League gradually reduced its role when other groups took partial responsibility, encouraging the demonstration project to find other support, and eventually it was turned over to the community. The county, in a bold choice, found a permanent home for the museum on that part of the Vizcaya property that used to produce livestock and vegetable gardens for the James Deering estate. With the help of those community leaders who envisioned what the museum could become for all of the chil-

Teaching a class on Indian migration at the Junior Museum, which became the Museum of Science and the Planetarium.

dren in the area, its growth continued, until even those who at first failed to grasp its potential changed their minds. Today we know this fledgling idea as the Planetarium and Museum of Science.

16

*P*ay the Toll

Lucy Cotton

The first island in the Venetian Causeway chain that includes Belle Isle, De Lido, San Marco, Rivo Alto, and San Marino was, for many years, simply a place where one encountered the tollbooth. For a long time after the causeway was opened in 1925, no houses were erected there; not a tree or structure marred the openness of the smooth white sand. But as the preferred islands beyond it were built up with luxury homes, and as moored yachts, like floating palaces, dotted the waterways, a residence was at last placed on the first in the chain, known as Biscayne Island. And for the next several years that single house stood, remarkable for its solitude, a sentinel surrounded by a flat expanse of fill bordered by the blue of the Intracoastal Waterway.

It was the home of Lucy Cotton Thomas, a colorful personality better known as Lucy Cotton Thomas Ament Hann McGraw Eristavi-Tchitcherine, that last name bringing a touch of deposed Russian nobility to her collection of six husbands. He also brought a (self-proclaimed) title of

"Prince"—or so her publicist said—and New York newspapers dutifully ran the photographs of their wedding in the Russian Orthodox cathedral there, capturing the moment in the ritual when double crowns were exchanged.

Though Lucy's husbands were many in number—one even making an encore in the role—only one had been a man of remarkable means. Edward Russell Thomas was the wealthy owner of the New York Morning Telegraph, which he had purchased from the estate of William Colins Whitney in the early 1900s. Thomas was a *bon vivant* of New York society whose keen interest in horseracing (he owned the famous racehorse Hermis), fast cars, and speed boats made his name well known in international circles as well. His sudden death in 1926, in the midst of divorcing Lucy Cotton but before the divorce became final, left his entire fortune in trust to their infant daughter, Lucetta. This trust became her

From Ziegfeld girl to princess: Lucy Cotton Thomas Ament Hann McGraw Eristavi-Tchitcherine.

mother's most dependable source of income.

By the time Lucetta was thirteen, she had reached the startling height of six foot one in her bare feet and was still growing. She was very shy but strong minded and was the *raison d'être* behind most requests from the large trust left by her father. (Gossip had it that the income from that fortune was reckoned by the day, not the year.) In truth, some of those requests might have seemed to benefit others besides Lucetta, but, as her mother reminded everyone, Lucetta was an heiress and, as such, entitled to all the associated perks whether she wanted them or not. A proper lifestyle, in today's vernacular. Nevertheless, Lucetta was indeed a very rich young woman, and Lucy Cotton Thomas found herself the mother of a gold mine.

A rather lonely girl, Lucetta was fiercely guarded by her remaining parent and by the Irving Trust of New York. Exercising their rightful authority, officials from the latter paid regular visits to the school where she was enrolled, meeting her friends and teachers in the course of their duties as trustees. The power of approval was forever being exercised.

Monies could be released on Lucetta's behalf for suitable housing (which, coincidentally, her mother used for lavish entertaining) and even a yacht for cruising (also used for entertaining), although Lucetta herself hated boats and was prone to seasickness. Notwithstanding, "an heiress must have a yacht, you know," said her mother, so a beautiful, white-and-mahogany, fifty-six-foot cruiser lay at anchor off the sea wall of the Biscayne Island villa.

The cream-colored house at 943 Venetian Drive, built in an L shape, sat behind its low bougainvillea-covered wall. A tiled loggia led past the front patio garden and into the small foyer. From there, one entered a white-and-gold main drawing room and dining room with white marble floors and picture windows. Both rooms faced northward on the bay, a view that might provide a glimpse of Guy Lombardo or Gar Wood racing a roaring speedboat in large circles on sunny winter mornings. A study, kitchen, and pantry completed the ground-floor design.

These rooms were not exceptionally large—barely villa-size, in fact—but the landscape beyond the picture windows was wonderful compensation. Serene water land undulated up the Intracoastal Waterway, the silhouettes of estates and small islands marking its shores as it spread northward. And above all that, of course, were Miami's matchless skies.

On the second floor, reached by circular staircase, were the master suite, three other bedrooms and baths, and a separate apartment over the loggia at the front of the house. This cloistered, inviolate space was Lucetta's, where she could listen to her jazz records and practice her clarinet far into the night.

Along with the new, Mediterranean-style villa and the sleek, mahogany-trimmed white yacht came eleven pet dogs—eleven different sizes and breeds and eleven different barks—that had free run of the house. In the driveway sat a chauffeur-driven black limousine, the kind with a speaker in a satin pocket in the back and a glass partition behind the driver, a dated idea of elegance, better suited to a more formal town than Miami, but perhaps the proper option in this setting. Though its use to Lucetta was chiefly for trips to and from school, music lessons, and doctors' appointments (her specialist at that time was a little Egyptian naturopath who treated her with vitamins, a newly discovered health regimen), it fit the heiress image and from that point of view seemed almost a necessity.

With the stage set and props in place, Christmastime, with its spirit of giving, offered Lucy Cotton the chance to become Lady Bountiful. The script called for her to set forth settled on the back cushions of the black limousine, the chauffeur's side filled with baskets of seasonal fruit. As she regally waited in her car, eyes straight ahead, he delivered these provisions to the doors of favored homes, along with her gold-engraved card surmounted by double crowns. Not everyone was filled with the Christmas spirit by this magnanimous gesture. One very annoyed recipient was heard to mutter at the chauffeur's departing back that it made him feel like a serf on a feudal estate. The gift-minus-the-giver syndrome.

This air of grandeur was in direct contrast to the personality of Lucy's next-to-last husband, William McGraw, a red-faced, overweight bully who had been, it was said, a promoter of prizefights in his younger days. Nevertheless, coming up in the world agreed with him. He enjoyed yachting on Lucetta's craft, standing on deck with legs splayed to brace against its motion, a big Cuban cigar in his beefy hand, describing those watching the boat's passage from the shore as "the proletariat." He repeated it so often it seemed to be a new word he was very proud of learning.

Somehow Lucetta survived in this odd milieu, though not with much enthusiasm. Impatient with the role in life she had been called upon to play, she was an extremely intelligent and artistic girl with a serious expression, a classic profile, and a tumble of tawny hair above a high forehead. Besides boats, she disliked the parties given by her mother, gatherings of wannabes and never-will-bes. These guests were the kind of people—never in short supply around the wealthy—who

The author and the "heiress" with one of her eleven dogs.

often depended on the lavish buffets at such events to sustain themselves on slim, between-patron incomes. They were always available to "fill in" if food was offered.

At one such occasion, the original Flapper Fanny, then in advanced years, was a guest and the subject of much curiosity. This icon from the past, darling of the Jazz Age and John Held drawings (in which she appeared blonded and skeletal), was rumored to have tattooed the color on her rosy lips and darkened eyebrows. It was also widely (or wildly) speculated that she injected wax under her wrinkles to smooth her skin, a treatment that needed frequent freshening as the wax tended to melt without warning (this in a time when lipstick was still considered a little daring). Disconcerting, to say the least.

When escape from her mother's parties was possible, Lucetta headed for her room, filling the solitary hours playing her clarinet (just a beginner), painting in oils (she showed great originality in technique, sometimes simply squeezing the paint directly from the tube onto the canvas), and collecting old jazz records, of which she had a formidable treasure. In truth, this intriguing new world of music became her obsession. She had them all—early Bix Beiderbecke, King Oliver, Jelly Roll Morton, Billie Holiday, Sydney Bechet—many of them rarities available only from collectors or on special order. Huge stacks of records in her closets left little room for clothes and spilled out onto the floor, as dozens of new ones arrived each month.

Even in summer, when her mother insisted she leave her records and accompany her on cruises to the Mediterranean or spend a month at the Lido in Italy (Would the trustees fund such trips otherwise?), her only interests seemed to be the ship's orchestra and the art museums they visited.

Occasionally, snippets about Lucetta appeared in Walter Winchell's column, mysterious to her and puzzling to her young classmates, whose lives were not troubled by tabloid items. "He said I had my hair done someplace famous in New York. I don't even know where it is. I've never been to the restaurant he said he saw me in!" she complained in disgust. In retrospect, it is not unlikely these items were planted by her mother's publicist (I suppose every heiress had one in those days). After all, Brenda Diana Duff Frazier had broken that taboo and reigned as Deb of the Year. But it annoyed Lucetta, who loathed the falseness of it all and the attention that inevitably followed.

Lucetta's best friend in the house on Venetian Drive was the cook, Siphronia, a kindly black woman of ample proportions who was a wonderful cook and, more important, the only one in that dysfunctional household who shared some of Lucetta's interests. Siphronia used to slip up to Lucetta's room and tell her about some of the black singers and musicians on her records. She knew true stories about many of them and had even seen a few perform over the years. Lucetta looked forward to Siphronia's visits and anecdotes. They brought a touch of reality to the old records she treasured and the research she spent hours absorbing. Siphronia helped pass the time in the young girl's rather lonely, out-of-school existence, a life in which the number of friends she was allowed to see was strictly limited by her watchful mother.

So it was a rude shock when Lucetta realized one day that Siphronia was no longer a fixture in the kitchen. Investigation revealed that her mother's then-husband, Prince Vladimir, had suddenly fired the woman. Stunned and disbelieving, the tearful girl confronted her titled stepfather, demanding an explanation.

"She was far too fat, my dear," he answered imperturbably. "A sure sign she ate too much. She was costing us money! We can't have that, you know, so I let her go." Since the money he referred to was all Lucetta's to begin with, this only escalated her outrage, adding another grievance to slowly building tensions in that house. Nevertheless, Lucy Cotton, a woman not easily put off, ignored the worsening climate between her daughter and her husband, clung to her adopted royal status, and insisted on always being addressed as "Princess Lucy."

America in the 1930s encountered a flood of refugees with titles, some real, most bogus. These so-called royals adeptly converted their mystique to a means of support through lucrative marriages or liaisons. As Europe lost its kingdoms and courts in the trouble brewing in the two decades before World War II, unskilled royalty from White Russia, the Balkans, and Spain scurried to find a way to continue their former lifestyles. What better refuge than America, with its moneyed women and ignorance of noble lineage? And what better place in America than a resort watering hole like Miami, where horseracing, polo, yachting, and private clubs provided glamorous activities? Prince Mdivani of Russia, Prince Ali Khan, the Rospigliosis, and other lesser nobles were part of the new café society that was crowding out the older names: the Deerings, the Vanderbilts, the Tiffanys. Those families still came each win-

Local resident Prince Joel, claimant to the throne of the Assyro-Chaldeans.

ter but shunned the more publicized life. Still, when Barbara Hutton and Doris Duke collected titles through marriage in that decade, it seemed the modern thing to do. Lucy Cotton felt happily comfortable in that company.

Born in Texas, Lucy was a tall woman, statuesque and dramatic, and projected a larger-than-life, dominating personality. The actress in Lucy Cotton sought the spotlight on society's stage, but it was a reality that forever seemed to elude her in this low-key, tropical land of lotus-eaters. (Perhaps that page of the script had been lost?)

No one was really quite sure what her true background was; the stories were many and details varied according to the source. One version portrayed her as an actress/showgirl in New York when Thomas married her. Another placed her in nearly a dozen early silent movies, including *The Devil* in 1921 with George Arliss and Edmund Lowe. She was handsome, with magnificent, deep-set, dark eyes, and her voice had a beautiful timbre: she was hard to overlook in any setting. But her penchant for shaving her head and wearing different wigs according to the occasion shocked the local movers and shakers, and Miami society never felt really comfortable with her.

In the course of becoming a socialite, Princess Lucy imagined she had business acumen as well, and during this alternative fantasy, she became convinced that there was oil in commercial quantities in the Everglades. She invested in several exploratory test wells in Collier County. The oil *was* there, it so happened, but difficult to extract for commercial purposes.

Next, she purchased a tract of land on the western outskirts of Miami, where she envisioned a marvelous recreational development to be called Princess Park. That project filled her with endless enthusiasm, leading her attorney to caution his secretaries not to put through her interminable phone calls. The details of this scheme were hazy and it never actually reached the drawing board.

In still another business venture, Lucy acquired the old

Oil rig at typical wildcat test well near Forty-Mile Bend on the Tamiami Trail. It's similar to the one Lucy Cotton had drilled.

Oil crew at test well in the Everglades.

"The largest salt-water pool in the world" at the Macfadden-Deauville on the ocean. Lucy Cotton owned the hotel in the 1940s.

Macfadden-Deauville Hotel on Miami Beach. This white elephant had been formerly owned by Bernarr Macfadden, the health guru of the 1930s whose wedding there was attended by the barefoot "Goat Lady" and her pet goat, both well-known local curiosities. (And, naturally, the host served non-alcoholic punch.) This neglected relic, a magnificent property in its prime fabled around the world for its Olympic-size pool and oceanfront location, was later acquired by members of the Mob before its eventual demolition. The names Little Augie and Greasy Thumb come to mind. From health to wealth to stealth.

None of these business projects prospered, and Lucy Cotton turned her attention once again to the social scene, always a mixed metaphor in Miami, where amorphous groups of varying income, interests, and background all felt *their* circle was the most desirable. New money flourished here in the sun. The very rich who could not make the A lists in the older enclaves of Philadelphia or St. Louis or Boston could, with the right use of their fortunes, enjoy a certain prominence in Miami. Here, they were forgiven their often-inauspicious beginnings as caterers, mechanics with a sudden moneymaker brainstorm, or waitresses who married up.

Still, acceptance was uncertain. If local gossip can be relied upon (and sometimes gossip gets it right), Princess Lucy gave a dinner party at the Macfadden-Deauville one evening. Hand-delivered, gold-printed invitations reached a number of Miamians, most of rather slim acquaintance. Gold service graced the long table for the occasion; mounds of floral centerpieces complemented the damask cloth and napkins; and from her extensive jewel collection Lucy selected diamond rings, an elaborate necklace, and a tiara to mark the occasion. Unhappily for the hostess, however, the appointed hour came and went but none of the invitees showed. Miami society, it seemed, was just not ready to be summoned for such imperial entertaining.

The lovely Mediterranean villa off the Venetian Causeway, with its colorful though largely forgotten past, is still there today but hard to distinguish. Not only is it now masked by mature landscaping, but where it once sat aloof and alone, it has since been joined by many other homes on that side of the island, and chalk-white high-rise condos now proliferate to the south. Biscayne Island, once barren, is no longer the sole province of the tollbooth.

In the final chapter, the princess in this fairy tale did not have a happy ending. Lucy Cotton committed suicide in her bedroom in that villa in 1948. Her jewel collection, left to Lucetta, was refused.

17

Driving Through the Past

The Warwick Estate

Where the Grove ends to the south, Cocoplum Circle defines the boundary of Miami and a piece of Coral Gables to the south and east. Expansion during the late 1940s began to push development into the vast amount of vacant land stretching toward Perrine, land that hid a few isolated estates in its heavy jungle growth.

This was high-table land based on solid coral rock and covered in scrub and palmettos, where the wells spouted iron-tainted water, dynamite was needed to plant small trees, and saltwater intrusion was likely. What is today Cocoplum on its elevated ridge, where countless million-dollar homes have been built, was then a vast, empty tract owned by the Deering heirs. Sidewalks and lampposts from the boom years peered through its overgrown weeds, evidence of housing planned but never built. Tahiti Beach at its eastern point was the only reason for driving down its rough, coral-rock road.

Old Cutler Road wound south past the new Gables Estates development (where a dry acre could be bought then for $12,000; today's lots are $2 million and up) and Old Cutler Bay (all properties once belonging to Arthur Vining Davis), to the newly subdivided acreage of Snapper Creek, Gables-by-the-Sea, and Devonwood. Habitation at last was making its way down the rough trail that had once led to the Warwick property before Devonwood claimed it.

Along the way, behind untouched hammock growth, lay the simple home and studio of Ralph Humes, a metal sculptor of nature subjects whose workshop was fascinating to visit, and Journey's End (now its own subdivision by that name), the home with its separate observation tower that was purchased after World War II by the aforementioned Arthur Vining Davis, multimillionaire owner of Alcoa Aluminum. Though Mr. Davis loved the house, he wanted the layout reversed, and so he promptly built a mirror image of the residence, leaving the original in place.

At the end of Coconut Grove South, where Ingraham runs into Le Jeune Road, there is a short bridge that crosses the Coral Gables Waterway, joining the southward thrust of Old Cutler Road. This narrow canal is deceptively deep— thirty feet or more. It starts its journey as a small spring on the Biltmore Golf Course, makes its way underneath US 1 where manatees and their pups sometimes browse in its out-fall on the other side, and continues under several bridges before spilling out to the wide south bay.

Along this meandering passageway, a "water life" inde-pendent of life onshore exists. Those who live on its high, coral-rock plateaus learn to recognize boaters from upstream as they glide under bridges and along the little canyons. They become familiar with the yachts that pass several times a week, sometimes with small parties in progress, sometimes just heading out for a day of fishing. Friendly waves to those on the banks are returned, and there is camaraderie even though an identity may be only a name on the stern of a craft. In time, these water neighbors become an integral part of one's landed world, and one looks with interest to see if it was a good day for fishing or sunburn.

For excitement on such a trip, it would be hard to top the story of a friend of mine who had married into a prominent and wealthy Chicago family. Cruising with friends along this waterway one sunny afternoon, she nonchalantly let her hand hang over the railing of the boat. Unfortunately for her, the large emerald ring she was wearing was loose and, without warning, slipped off her finger and into the murky waters below. An intensive search for the precious gem was made by the insurance company, which sent divers to comb the dredged, deep coral-rock canal. But the gem was never recovered from that creviced canyon. Scuba diving, anyone?

Old Cutler, which follows that lofty limestone ridge along the bay south of Cocoplum Circle, has a stretch of rolling pavement where on soft summer nights kids used to skate by hanging onto the back bumpers of passing cars, then letting go. As good a way as any, I suppose, to get killed. That historic link to the past (once the trail of the Barefoot Mailman) rolled on down toward Snapper Creek Estates, past the lush acres of Fairchild Garden, then down to Black Point Marina, just south of the estate of Charles Deering, brother of James, who built Vizcaya. Such is the trail's importance to Miami's history that Old Cutler has been favored with its Historic Highway status and thus, to its credit and survival, can never be widened or changed.

At the south end of Old Cutler Road, where it meets 67th Avenue and 136th Street, lies an upscale subdivision known today as Devonwood. Here, luxury homes, well hidden from the traffic on Old Cutler, nestle in lush plantings, some of them part of the fruited groves put in by a former owner, John Warwick of Chicago, Illinois.

Back in the early 1920s, Mr. Warwick's doctor told him he had six months to live. Unfazed by this pronouncement, Mr. Warwick decided to come to south Florida, with his chauffeur at the wheel, to see if Miami's weather could help his health in the short time he had been told was left to him. He liked what he saw in the budding frontier—enthusiasm and opportunities in a growing town, mild winters—and he felt better in the sunny climate. He decided to stay.

He considered Miami Beach, which was seeing a frenzied boom in the buying and selling of oceanfront property. Property was sometimes sold, resold, and sold yet again in the same day. In fact, when title companies shut their doors at closing time, orders were still being thrown over the office transoms by frantic agents desperately hoping theirs would be the first abstract out the next day, before prices rose again.

But all that beach sand left John Warwick unimpressed. "You can't grow anything in that," he said dismissively, which was certainly true enough, and, turning his attention to the more agricultural end of the area, he purchased the parcel to be known for many decades as the Warwick Estate down on Old Cutler Road, about as far from the beach as one could get in those days without leaving the county. There he planted rows of fancy avocados and mangos, luxury produce that could be shipped to Northern markets each winter. In later years, as hotels mushroomed on Miami Beach and real estate prices climbed to the moon (publicist Steve Hannigan had invented the "bathing beauty" and created seemingly insatiable desire for the tropics), Mr. Warwick waited confidently for the land boom to move southward.

In truth, there was already lots of commercial activity south of the Warwick Estate, in the little town of Perrine. Back then, Perrine, Goulds, and Princeton had a flourishing lumber industry, which used a natural resource of Florida, the slash pine (Dade County pine was harvested into oblivion), to produce wood, turpentine, and resin. Tomato and potato growers, too, benefited from the good soil, flat, cleared land, and nonstop sunshine. Citrus groves found favor in the warm winters as well. Many growers at that time remembered the hard, killing freezes that sometimes plagued central Florida crops, causing devastating losses and sending growers southward.

On his new homestead, John Warwick, sometimes referred to by his friends as the unofficial mayor of Cutler, planted his income-producing groves of premium produce.

Some of these trees, happy with their care, eventually reached heights of twenty to thirty feet. For irrigation, a windmill was erected on the property to tap into well water produced by the natural springs, with which the area is rich. A thick windbreak of Australian pines was planted to keep the occasional cold, north winds from pinching buds that showed themselves in February. (It also served as a handy landmark when one got turned around in that area of palmetto and scrub pine.) Many of those fruit trees are still in place today, quietly drowsing among the beautiful homes that have raised their walls there, but the windmill is gone.

Warwick built a large residence on his land and settled there with his wife and two daughters. The Victorian country house was very spacious and originally looked out on the surrounding lush, green groves. Diamond-shaped mullions glittered in its casement windows that banked the broad front terrace, with its comfortable, wrought-iron furniture, a place to sit and enjoy the spill of yellow allamanda blossoms that cascaded over the stonework below. The huge drawing room running along the eastern exposure downstairs was filled with light by walls of French windows on three sides.

Windmill at the avocado groves on the Warwick property.

*Allamanda blooms spill
over the terrace of the
Warwick home on Old
Cutler Road.*

Long, well-proportioned, and paneled in warm brown wain-scoting, its spaciousness humbled the grand piano at one end. High, coffered white ceilings covered in beautiful plasterwork gave ambiance to the room. The intricate designs were the artistry, it was said, of a craftsman brought from Scotland especially for the task, who spent nearly a year fashioning the plasterwork's exquisite detail.

Northeast of the house, at the end of the porte-cochere and beside the garage that held a stately old Pierce Arrow up on blocks (with artificial flowers still in its small window vases above the hand straps with tassels), sat a small, screened cabana house. In the 1930s, a gray cement pool yawned before it, unfinished but usable, a witness to the bank failures of that decade. Savings that had been put aside to tile its rough concrete sides had vanished overnight (a common enough story then), leaving the pool resignedly waiting for its ceramic finishes. Though pool parties were never constrained by its lack of decoration (just don't come in contact with its bruising sides was the advice), the better times needed to complete the job were still some years away. Until then, it held water, which, after all, was its primary purpose.

Across the road from the Warwicks sat the flat, open, featureless acres of Chapman Field. Originally a World War I training airfield, it later became a USDA-owned property for studying plants in a subtropical environment as well as for introducing new agricultural species. It has not changed appreciably since then. Not much else was to be seen in that remote spot before World War II—no streetlights, buildings, or other signs of life. It was simply rural country, eerily dark and isolated at night, a few whip-poor-wills and lots of owls for company.

Locals used to tell tales of a marauding pirate, Black Caesar, whose haunting presence was rumored to still be in the area. Depending on which version one preferred, Black Caesar was either a runaway slave or a deposed African Prince who sailed the waters of Biscayne Bay and the Caribbean looking for ships to plunder and shipwrecks to salvage—vessels that might have been caught in hurricanes as they headed toward Spain with their heavy cargoes of gold and silver from Mexico and South America. Legend has it that Caesar and his band of brigands used to camp in the Cutler area, coming in after successful raids to divide the treasure stolen from the unlucky galleons that strayed from tropical shipping lanes only to founder on treacherous coral reefs. Their spoils buried, the pirates would refill their barrels with fresh water from a large spring once located there before setting sail again.

Strangely, these tales of piracy persist, though no treasure has ever been found. If such a trove ever existed and is now hidden somewhere under the tangled mangroves or indestructible palmettos nearby, it may sleep forever, for in today's world, these environmentally sensitive areas cannot be disturbed. Black Caesar's only legacy thus far is his name on maps today showing Caesar's Creek.

Later, Black Caesar's Forge, a trendy, open-air restaurant—where they slow-cooked baking potatoes in a huge pot of bubbling resin, wrapped them in twists of newspaper, and served them with grilled prime steaks without equal—opened on that spot. The heady mix of the aromas of smoking resin and grilled meat and the light of candles and cooking fires made one's dining experience romantic and memorable. Today we know the area as the King's Bay subdivision. Alas, the restaurant is gone, Black Caesar has not returned, and though I doubt there is a spadeful of unturned earth in Gables-by-the-Sea, Paradise Point, or King's Bay, the legend persists.

Residing so far from the madding crowd in Miami did not deter Mr. Warwick's party-loving teenage daughters from enjoying an active social life and the company of other young people. It did present a problem, however, for the young men they dated. Dreading that long drive down remote Old Cutler Road to bring the girls home after an evening's social event, they sometimes furtively drew straws for the unappetizing duty.

The Warwick girls, noted among their friends for ordering their lives according to numerology and astrology, occasionally faced the task of driving themselves from the Coral Gables Waterway to SW 136th Street alone at night. Mindful of that ill-defined, dark road that wound through the area's dense growth (Matheson Hammock is all that remains now), they prepared for possible encounters with nature's wildlife. The road, not too visible even in daylight, was almost impenetrably dark at night and covered with startled night creatures caught in a car's headlights. In the rainy season, especially, the road seemed literally paved with blue land crabs vacating their flooded homes for the higher ground of the ridge. Like grotesque ballerinas, these awkward creatures tiptoed across the rough path. Raising their claws in defiance, they scuttled into the mangroves by the hundreds, making a harsh rustling noise as their shells grazed the underbrush. The crabs were a concern to be taken very seriously. It was well known to locals that the crustaceans' knife-sharp shells, when crushed, could easily slash or puncture one's tires. And a flat tire in that area was to be avoided, if at all possible, since hardly a soul who might be of help passed that way after dark.

In addition, the very remoteness of the area gave it a dubious reputation, not wholly undeserved. Among the local population it was rumored that the stretch of dark beach along the bay sometimes afforded perfect cover for less-than-wholesome activities. Rumrunning at that time was a thriving occupation for some (including a woman known in local courts as the Queen of the Bootleggers). The numerous shallow coves up and down that length of bay shore invited the easy smuggling of stolen goods. And illegal immigrants found landing there convenient and satisfactorily secluded. In essence, it was a location best left to those who had business there, and it was certainly not a good place for car trouble.

Nevertheless, undeterred by these obstacles and determined not to miss out on any social activities, Mr. Warwick's daughters devised their own safety measures. They made a

Mangroves, hidden harbors for smugglers.

stuffed figure with a pillow for a head and dressed it in men's clothing. This formidable companion rode shotgun with them in the front seat of their car as they started into that dark tunnel of trees, their father's hats pulled down over their pinned-up hair. Perhaps their ruling planets were in the right house during those trips or they were spelling their names that year with the correct number of letters, for nothing happened to interrupt them on their social rounds, and as human habitation began to invade that long stretch of original hammock, tensions eased and 136th Street seemed not so far away.

It wasn't all danger and foreboding along that lonely ridge. One very hot July night, the sisters hosted a pajama party with friends. To cap the evening, the group all piled into the Warwicks' wood-sided station wagon. Relying on safety in numbers, they headed down to Tahiti Beach for a breath of cool air. Today this is the most exclusive part of Cocoplum, but then it was only a wide, white-sand beach with little thatched huts and sunshades and a steel shark net (which didn't keep out the baby sharks, which swam through the netting and grew bigger inside, near the beach).

Tahiti Beach in the 1920s: white sand (unlike Miami Beach) and a steel shark net. Today multimillion dollar residences abound.

The crowd of sillies sang as the wheels spun on the crushed rock road, and they shot off firecrackers and tossed them from the back of the car into the brooding mangroves. No sentry gates at Cocoplum on that rough, bumpy road then, no lights, no houses, no one to hear or care. Ah, youth! Ah, wilderness!

Oh, yes. John Warwick, the unofficial mayor of Cutler? He outlived by many years both his Chicago doctor and that pessimistic physician's dire prediction of six short months.

18

Sand Bytes

Miami of the '30s

In the 1920s and 1930s, you had to bring them with you to Miami if you had a desire for serious luxuries. Residents who were used to the choices found in larger markets ordered their furniture from New York or Europe, their fashions from Rich's in Atlanta or Boule Miche in Chicago. There were no boutiques or branches from Fifth Avenue or Madison Avenue to tempt one. Local stores still carried primarily what appealed to year-round residents. Without the climate control of air conditioning we enjoy today, Miami's trade winds dictated lightweight clothing, bright-colored or pale accessories, and pastel house furnishings. Cutting-edge or very traditional taste bowed inevitably to what could survive the heat and humidity.

Very gradually Miami found its own special appeal. And that was a look designed for the sophisticated traveler whose home city did not offer "winter resort fashions." Rather than heavy wools, the emphasis was on warm weather wardrobes, elegant high style for a warm winter season, suitable for cruising or the social life of the tropics. Burdine's featured an annual "Sand in Your Shoes" print, which appeared on bags, shoes, dresses, and hats, and with each new design the store urged "Bring Your Trunks Empty." Women took up golf and its appropriate garb; cabana pajamas were approved day wear at the beach clubs; and the races, nightclubs, and sports events required apparel specifically designed for each activity. No one-size-fits-all-T-shirt-and-jeans look. Style aced comfort every time.

In fact, image, especially the appearance of being modern or sophisticated, was a powerful tool of the public relations media. It was the siren call of ads and newspaper stories urging tourists to visit a place where the most up-to-date ideas ensured that one was "in the know." And it was effective.

The late 1920s and 1930s were caught up in the words *Art Deco* and *streamlined* and *modern*. Automobile manufacturers chose model names like Airflow, Zephyr, and Fluid Drive to describe their cars' attributes. Trains had names like *Silver Meteor* and the *Orange Blossom Special* (a Yankee friend thought the latter must be a honeymoon train, but then she also thought kumquats were baby oranges). Newly built trains mirrored the new cross-country liners, such as the sleek, silvery *Twentieth Century Limited*. That icon, featured in Hollywood films, made travel a glamorous adventure and conjured up the romance and possibilities of new horizons. Contemporary houses and apartment buildings, washed in delicate pastel colors, sprouted concrete eyebrows, clean lines, rounded corners, glass bricks, and that curious punctuation, the porthole, which was usually a dead give-away for the location of a bathroom.

Reflecting this pride in the new and optimistic, Miami was becoming predominately a city of young people. It offered them a chance to influence a growing community open to innovative ideas. The small hometowns or farms they came from often had customs entrenched in the past. Miami, on the other hand, offered a fresh start in uncharted territory with untried ways of approach. Freed from bad weather and cities grimed with coal dust, young people

Couple in fancy dress at one of the masquerade balls in the 1920s.

moved here in impressive numbers, bringing their enthusiasm, determination to succeed, and a sense of fun.

Swimming casinos, ferry rides, masquerade parties, the Charleston, and parades down Flagler Street gave an amusement-park slant to 1920s Miami. A common sight were the Binder Boys, real estate agents in straw boaters who accepted a nominal deposit to "bind" a real estate deal. They exhorted the crowds to buy before prices went up as they rode crepe paper–strewn flatbeds down Miami's main street. (There were actually real estate agents among the very first few settlers.)

Dirigibles floating over the city, horseracing at Hialeah, greyhounds at West Flagler, Aerocars, and the craze for Latin

music and the Rhumba marked the 1930s as Hollywood
sent us Carmen Miranda and "Flying Down to Rio" with
dancers on the wings of a plane. The advent of retirees on
pensions in the brand new Art Deco hotels along Ocean
Drive was a notion too far-fetched to contemplate. The
excitement of South Beach in the 1990s, though on a much
more sophisticated scale, was not unlike the mood back
then—youthful, relaxed, and exhilarating with a fun-in-the-
sun attitude.

Along with its pleasant pastimes, however, Miami
attracted its share of corruption, both local and imported
from older cities in the North and Midwest. Opportunities
for fraud were everywhere for those practiced in such arts.
From the first swampland manipulators in the city's earliest
days, to the rumrunners during Prohibition, to the wide-
spread gambling and bookie joints so prevalent in the 1930s,
the shady travelers came every winter to the resort where
money and speculators were plentiful. They discovered they
could combine a winter vacation with the invention of new
scams, often perfecting their schemes here, then introducing
the polished versions to the larger venues of New York or
Chicago. These hucksters were also quick to realize that the
transient nature of the community made them less conspic-
uous and more difficult to find and punish on discovery. It
was all the encouragement they needed.

When gangster Al Capone resided on Palm Island (his
son went to school at St. Patrick's on the Beach), the unwrit-
ten agreement among crime figures was that the town would
be a neutral space where mobsters could vacation in safety
from gang wars and a truce would be observed. Honor
among thieves. This hope vanished when shadowy bagmen
appeared, carrying illegal payoffs to local politicians.
Growing suspicions of mobster activity were borne out
when the Silver Slipper supper club on the outskirts of town
was raided. The surprise visit was instigated by the office of
the city prosecutor, whose star at that time was a crusading
young attorney named George Smathers. Seized evidence

revealed the underground network of gambling and prosti-
tution that had moved into the area, and behind the on-stage
celebrity entertainment, the criminal element hovered in the
wings. (Building on the high visibility of that particular case,
Smathers' career headed for the halls of Congress, where he
served as senator for many years.)

In still other raids, illegal slot machines (the popular
"one-armed bandits") were seized and warehoused and
bookie joints busted, and it became increasingly worrisome
that racketeers, always looking for profitable new business to
control, had moved south to the shores of Biscayne Bay. The
whispers of corruption, now becoming loud and clear, at one
point indicated possible involvement reaching as far as the
governor's mansion in Tallahassee.

Not that discovery ended the problem; it just confirmed
it. As late as the war years, branches of the Purple Gang of
Detroit and Murder, Inc. established a foothold in Miami,
though their quiet entry was soon shouted in the local newspapers. It was no surprise to anyone years later when Senator
Estes Kefauver held his crime investigation hearings in the
town. There was a lot going on. At one point, Miami's newspapers, caricaturing local officials in a series of political car-
toons, dubbed a particular city commission of the 1930s
"The Termite Administration." Members were notorious for
quietly undermining legitimate government while they lined
their own pockets as law enforcement looked the other way.

Despite the parallel undercurrent of corruption, a sense
of heady optimism continued to persevere, producing grand
schemes for real estate development before the deepening
Depression all across the country began to grind down the
more ebullient spirits. Miami Beach, having risen from a spit
of mangroves and mosquitoes to a city of beautiful homes
and golf courses, was a striking demonstration of what could
be accomplished when men like Flagler, Fisher, and Merrick,
visionaries all, made the apparently impossible happen. It
seemed that just a dream and publicity were sufficient to
bring new visitors this far south.

By the time the 1930s came into view, tall office build-ings had been erected and waited confidently for new busi-nesses sure to come. The Coliseum was built on Douglas Road (where the Oberammergau Passion play was subse-quently performed one year) with visions of sports events in mind. It would later become an ice rink. The Hialeah Fronton brought jai alai, a Basque game with Basque players and betting—the only one in this country. Miles of sidewalk were poured where no house stood, complete with street-lights and fire hydrants, poised for future development. Greyhound racing out on West Flagler brought with it huge grandstands waiting for overflow crowds. Venetian gondo-liers poling in the canals of the Gables, fox hunting parties tally-hoing across golf courses (where even today a live fox can be found)—nothing seemed too far-fetched for people's aspirations. Expectations were high and confidence soared. By the summer of 1926, the 1920s did indeed roar.

But the one-two punch of the '26 hurricane and the fallout in land prices after the stock market debacle three years later stunned the city. Those absentees who had pur-chased lots above and underwater abandoned their owner-ship by the hundreds, unwilling to pay taxes on land they could not afford to visit. This led to so much fraud and con-fusion in the conveyance of property and delinquency of taxes that the idea of title insurance made sense.

In the sobering years of the Depression that followed, bargains mushroomed everywhere. Oceanfront lots were going for $5,000, down from million-dollar figures for choice locations. The Congress Building downtown, thirteen stories of empty office space, found a buyer for less than $20,000. A fully furnished, two-story, Spanish-style house in the Gables, silver and linens included, could be rented for $25 a month. For Sale signs got larger and larger, almost bill-board size, until the city of Coral Gables finally enacted a law determining the smaller size you see today. In the course of time, the signs stayed small—but not the prices.

Money for development in this community had always

come from outside the state, and Northern banks had been badly shaken by the potential for damage from hurricanes. There were enough problems from the failures of banks across the country without sending money to be blown away by storm-force winds. The end result was that the city's forward motion of expansion came to a halt as the whole country faced more serious problems of survival. Nevertheless, though abandoned by all but the very rich (the sun and the sea never change), life here drifted forward, its prosperity compromised, waiting uncertainly for the economy to recover—for the boom days to return.

But a different scenario was being written. When America entered World War II, Miami was asked to play an important role in the training of the military, a role for which its weather, water, and empty hotels made it the perfect choice. And the city gratefully rose to the challenge.

19

W *ar and Peace*

1941–1950

When the effects of World War II began to be felt in Miami, everything changed. The tempo of docks, offices, and airfields increased as the town became a military troop training and rehabilitation center. Private parties got smaller due to gas rationing, food restrictions, and a new problem: where did one get help to do all this? Everyone, it seemed, had a part to play in the war effort and was off somewhere spotting planes, rolling bandages, or censoring mail. Some residents past draft age activated their reserve officer status and went packing. Others leased their homes to new government big-wigs and took up residence at one of the downtown apartment hotels—the Granada, Dallas Park, or The Towers—or just went fishing for the duration.

Miami and Miami Beach hotels were stripped of their luxurious furnishings, their windows painted black so no light could be seen from the sea. Overnight they became high-rise barracks for enlisted men and quarters for their officers. The Municipal Golf Course of Miami Beach served

Apartment hotels along the north side of the Miami River. They were a way of life that provided hotel services to apartment dwellers.

as an Officers Training School drill field for the likes of Clark Gable and other visiting celebrities who now were working for Uncle Sam. At midday on Dade Boulevard, traffic often came to a halt as long, marching lines of young men crossed in arm-swinging cadence to the golf course, where one could see them performing calisthenics and marching drills. The skies seemed full of low-flying craft, and one only hoped an instructor was carefully monitoring the student pilots. In the evening, two lone buglers stationed on the top floors of the old Floridian and Flamingo Hotels at the Beach end of the County Causeway faced each other and sounded taps—haunting notes that hung suspended in the heavy, tropical air. In every aspect of daily life, Miami was two cities, the permanent one and the ever-changing military one.

Where glittering Bal Harbor rises today, only sea gulls and empty banks of sand dunes covered with tall sea grass existed, making it the perfect spot for a practice rifle range. Because Miami was a coastal city and thus vulnerable to invasion by sea, blackouts were ordered and the headlights of any cars out after dark had to be taped in black to cut down their beams under penalty of arrest. (Did you know

*Training flight over Miami.
Lots of air traffic during
World War II.*

that one government plan called for not defending Florida south of Jacksonville? Too much coastline to cover!) It was impressed upon citizens that the glow of an ember from a lit cigarette could be seen from three miles high. Volunteers patrolled the beaches at night on horseback, watching for potential invasion by sea. The city became headquarters for the U.S. Coast Guard, the U.S. Navy Sub-Chaser School, the Redistribution Center for returning veterans waiting to be reassigned, and pilot training for the Royal Air Force. Young men of the Russian navy came one summer to study sonar, the new device that located enemy submarines by a series of echoes bounced off the ocean bottom. It was a technical procedure that remained a mystery to them for most of the war, according to some of their classmates.

All of these schools and training classes had to be geared up as quickly as possible to amass a fighting force from so many branches of the services and from the civilian population. Miami, along with other cities that stayed warm through the winter, was an important hub for this task. Miamians played a vital part in plane-spotting, and the city

was a major censor center for incoming and outgoing overseas mail. As the "ninety-day wonders" were churned out by
the Officers Training School, the luxurious Biltmore Hotel,
whose days until then had seen only relaxation and pamper-
ing for the rich, became a stark and efficient Veterans
Hospital for the returning wounded. Bandages were rolled
ad infinitum, long scarves and sweaters grew from busy needles, and street corners blossomed with big barrels painted
red, white, and blue and labeled "Bundles for Britain." In a
burst of patriotic fervor, the idea was put forth that all the
fireplugs should be painted red, white, and blue too, but
then someone realized that would make it harder for fire-
men to locate the plugs in times of emergency.

Unlike today's ringside TV seats, from which one can
get a look at the latest secret weapons or actual combat and
troop movements at the click of a remote, news of World
War II was tightly controlled. Today's wars have become
entertainment and have lost the tension and gravity felt back
then. During World War II, information came only from the
Pentagon. Reading between the lines of V-mail (short gov-
ernment-sent missives bearing no telltale postmark) and
guessing where someone might be stationed was a frustrating (but understandable) sort of correspondence. Loose lips
could indeed sink ships, and no one wanted that.

Here on the home front, though, there were gossipy
news items that happened on our doorstep, a welcome relief
from all the concern that occupied our minds. One day, sub-
marine-spotting ships from the Sub-Chaser School went out
toward the Gulf Stream, as they did every day, to practice
searching for the enemy. On that memorable trip, they were
nearly three miles offshore when one of the naval crew
heard the sonar sound the alarm, indicating a very long
metal object in the water below. Excitement ran high among
the junior officers onboard, who had not had any live action
experience in service up to this point. Briefings, of course,
had made them well aware of reports of Nazi subs lurking
close to the Florida coastline and Gulf Stream shipping

lanes. These marauding "Wolf Packs," having lost some of their effectiveness in the North Atlantic, soon found bases in South America and had begun to focus on the Eastern seaboard of the United States.

So it was with a sense of the very real possibility of the presence of the enemy that the order was hurriedly given to release the torpedoes. The resulting explosions, powerful and loud, brought forth huge amounts of debris to the surface, confirming a direct hit. The jubilant shouts of victory were cut short, however, when it slowly dawned on the crew that it was not wreckage from a German sub that dotted the bay waters around them. Rather, the churning debris indicated a far more serious target had been hit. The might of the United States Navy had managed to torpedo the Miami sewage system main outfall pipe instead!

Nevertheless, we civilians were glad our sailors were so alert. One local news story reported that German gear and

Freighter hit by German sub in 1942 off Miami. Courtesy of the Historical Museum of Southern Florida

even ticket stubs from the Olympia Theater (now Gusman Hall) were found on local mangrove sand spits. And if you doubted the enemy's presence was too close for comfort, there was, on several occasions, an ominous red glow clearly visible on the horizon at night. Intercepted transport supply steamers and oil tankers were sometimes torpedoed in the shipping lanes where they plodded, helpless and slow, attractive targets for the enemy. When attacked by Nazi U-boats, their fires blazed for hours in the darkness several miles offshore, leaving an ugly red bruise on the horizon and giving further proof that the war was not confined to the shores of Europe or Asia.

Late one afternoon on Biscayne Boulevard, the city had an unexpected treat. In front of the Everglades Hotel, which then served as a barracks for sailors of the Russian navy, passersby heard a haunting chorus of male voices floating in the air above the park and its bayfront. Looking up at the half-opened windows on the eighteenth floor, one could see the faces of fifty or more Russian sailors as they leaned far out over the narrow sills. Perhaps feeling a little homesick, they had spontaneously burst forth with the stirring melody of their own national anthem, "Meadowland." As its deep notes of melancholy soared and swelled above the street below, one could almost believe their Mother Russia could hear her sailors calling from across the sea. Unforgettable!

Unforgettable, too, was the day traffic was tied up (as usual), waiting for the Brickell Avenue drawbridge to close behind a vessel going upriver. As traffic idled (using precious gas), I noticed in the lane to my right a huge trailer towing a one-man Japanese submarine, a little suicide craft that called for certain sacrifice. Inside sat a small figure, staring straight ahead. This was closer to the enemy than I really wanted to be. After a few moments of nervousness, logic took over and I exhaled, realizing it had to be a captured sub with a dummy in place, probably on its way to some training course or exhibition.

With so much government money floating around and

Old postcard locating Miami Beach hotels taken over by the government for barracks. At least the recruits got great views!

so few goods to spend it on, nightclubs and restaurants flourished. They seemed able to get the scarcities the average citizen found only in the ration books or not at all. They provided celebrity headliners, good food, and music, and enabled those with uncertain destinations to relax a little.

Photograph frame from the Clover Club on Biscayne Boulevard.

The Clover Club was where the new comedy team of Dean Martin and Jerry Lewis bombed, but the owner kept them on because they made *him* laugh. Popular too were Club Bali, The Little Palm (where discreet gambling was available), Bill Jordan's Bar of Music (where "all night long the glasses tinkle"), Five O'Clock, Rhumba Casino, the Latin Quarter (which was owned by Lou Walters, Barbara's father, and which sat in the center of Palm Island and later burned to the ground), and the Beachcomber on Dade Boulevard (later to become a crematorium), to name a few. Desi Arnaz, an early teenage exile from Cuba, where his father had once been a high government official, no longer cleaned birdcages or gave guitar lessons when he went from playing bongos in local night spots to Broadway, where he made his mark in the musical hit *Too Many Girls*.

The private clubs either closed for the duration of the war or curtailed parties but left their cabanas open to members. In the case of the Bath Club and the Surf Club, their membership policies were suspended and they welcomed some of the military brass, who were the celebrities of that time. Sunday buffets at the clubs never seemed to lack roast beef and other goodies. Perhaps these were scenes similar to the British colonial life in India and Hong Kong. Officers and their ladies mingled easily with the local residents, although the shadow of war was always lurking in the corners. But an excuse for gaiety in such times could certainly be justified as keeping up the spirits of those on their way to new assignments. After all, who knew how long before they returned home? Unspoken was the somber thought *or if?*

And so, unlike other cities, where people simply marked time until normal life could be resumed, Miami was neither deserted nor devoid of activity. Still, as the song went, those men who were still here were "either too young or too old" or 4F (or, as some claimed, "I'm in civilian clothes because I'm *really* a secret agent."). Those in uniform who were on shore duty commandeered LMDs, or Large Mahogany Desks, in the duPont Building, a choice assignment. There were so many administrative offices for both military and civil defense workers that Flagler Street at lunchtime was a sea of whites, khaki uniforms, and gold braid, all snappily saluting their way down the street. The Hotel Urmey, with its second-floor veranda lined with rocking chairs overlooking SE 1st Street, was a popular downtown eating spot fondly known as "The Wormy" to locals. Even Burdine's Tea Room saw its share of brass and their dates.

Important military figures came and went without fanfare on hush-hush visits. One afternoon at the Surf Club cabanas, I noticed a tall, very handsome, mustached and beetle-browed Scotsman in bonnet, kilt, and high socks, gazing out at the waves. He was obviously preoccupied watching a figure floating just offshore in the gentle ocean surf. All I could see from that distance was a large stomach serenely bobbing above the waves and the tip of a lit cigar. The bather must be important, I surmised, even for these grand surroundings, where prominent guests from all over the world appear each season without special treatment. Eventually, the chubby figure with the face of a baby beached itself and was wrapped head to toe in capacious toweling by his sentry. Then, with a friendly wave of his cigar, he strolled off toward the clubhouse, followed by the watchful Scotsman. Did you guess Winston Churchill and his security? Right!

When the war finally ended, Miami caught its breath and braced for a new kind of invasion. Men who had been stationed here at one time or another during the war had fallen for the clean air, the warm winters, and the opportunities they saw around them. Having glimpsed how the denizens of paradise lived, they wanted to be a part of that lifestyle. The war had uprooted many men who might never have left their ties to other parts of the country, and traveling had become second nature to them. So they returned to the Magic City by the bay—this time to stay, find a home, and raise their families.

Some changes that had been on hold during the war now began to take place. The days were numbered for the dangerously exposed Florida East Coast Railway track that crossed downtown Flagler Street on the west side of the courthouse back then, often holding up busy traffic for greater parts of the day and once even delaying for hours spectators on their way to an Orange Bowl parade. Limited, too, was the time remaining for the old, gray stone, two-story police station with double-hung windows across from the courthouse, which was no longer adequate to serve the spreading community, and for the fire station next door to it, which disgorged its two lumbering engines onto Flagler Street—a very dangerous situation. Inspired by the magnificent new Alfred I. duPont bank and office building downtown (completed just before the war), whose marble and bronze finishes and two-story escalators were amazing to the locals, other buildings put on new faces. Eventually, hotels were reconverted and totally refurbished with funds from the federal government now that the trainees and officers were gone. Moviemakers discovered anew the sun, surf, and

Frank Sinatra (center) shooting the movie Tony Rome *on Bayshore Drive off Brickell Avenue in the 1950s.*

greenery. Tourists came back in even greater numbers. Though there was no way to discourage the buzzards that arrived at the top of the courthouse every autumn (the updrafts caused by the stepped tower made it the perfect spot for gliding), Orange Blossom perfume was no longer the only scent to be found in the tourist shops. Miami was poised to expand!

Many newcomers found house hunting after the war difficult, however. Existing housing was outrageously expensive compared to what prices had been (though the mortgage rate was 4.5%), and new dwellings were often built from 1938 house plans, not incorporating any of the new materials and advances in construction discovered by the war effort. Building supplies were hard to find. New owners sometimes had to settle for blue tinted-glass windows, green timber that split or warped, and even mismatched colors in plumbing fixtures, depending on what was sitting in the warehouses. Nevertheless, it was home, and they happily put down roots.

Essex Village in Hialeah was one of the first of the new developments. The homes came with flat roofs, a carport (no garage), and a newly invented Bendix washing machine as a bonus, all for $8,000–12,000. South of South Miami, in what is today the village of Pinecrest, rose Martin's Suburban Acres (or, as some referred to it, "Bourbon Acres" because of refreshments at all the barbecue parties that were becoming the rage). Those houses, with fireplaces and an acre of land, ran $11,000–16,000. Today, an acre alone sells for $375,000 and up!

With new houses that grew bigger and more luxurious as the years passed came a different kind of homeowner, the corporate executive, who could put most of his lifestyle on an expense account. Professionals, too, enjoyed a larger bite of the economy, and "consulting" became a road to riches. These newly arrived residents contributed to local charities and paved the way for new schools, churches, and community improvements. Their contributions changed Miami into a "big" city. The community grew larger and more sophisticated—physically, socially, and economically. Volunteers and club groups surrendered many of their tasks to paid workers. Professional fundraising, staffed charities, and the benefits of networking established the new standards for moving forward. If the inevitable result of this surge of newcomers was that they had less knowledge of more neighbors, it was something that was happening everywhere else in the country as well.

Wisely, Miami did not abandon its long-held image as a city of leisure pursuits. It remained a tropical resort for visitors to relax and have fun. But other more serious reasons for coming here were offered. Commercial and corporate opportunities expanded. New ways of building on our infrastructure were developed. A better understanding of the uniqueness of the Everglades and its importance to our survival emerged. The excitement of the undersea world off our shores waited to be explored. The city's strategic location for trade and travel in this hemisphere became increasingly obvious. It was manifest destiny for Miami.

With so much happening in such a short span of time, traffic became a nightmare, with insufficient and poorly marked roads and intersections and no expressways, flyovers, Metrorail, or people movers to connect the new suburbs with the centers of downtown. Those who had lived here for years and enjoyed a more relaxed lifestyle deplored the frantic pace of it all. They wanted to turn the clock back to a simpler time. But, like it or not, like Mario Andretti we were racing full speed ahead. The war had ended, and the second half of the twentieth century beckoned, along with unfinished college courses, new ways of doing things, and the arrival of the Golden Fifties.

Would we be the true commercial city we are today or still only a pleasure resort if the war had not touched us in the ways that it did? In my view, sooner or later Miami was destined to be discovered anew as it was by those early visitors who stayed. Thanks to those in the first wave, whose presence still marks the shelters they built and left for others to inherit and whose confidence in the future of Miami never wavered, that promise was becoming a reality. The flying boats at Dinner Key no longer arrived, but Miami's location as the natural link between North America and South America made its role inevitable. The word was out. Miami was again the place to be.

20

Loose Leaves

Vignettes

Here and there, small images from Miami's past come to mind—brief, sharp vignettes, gone in a flicker but telling in their reality. As an artist may complete his canvas with the casual details that somehow bring truth to his work, so remembered fragments can cross the T's and dot the I's of a recollection. They are metaphors for a bit of time that informs the larger portrait, enduring reminders of yesterday. These are mine.

• • •

The house at the northeast corner of 15th Road and Brickell (now an office building's footpad), where one fanciful owner painted the ceiling of the master bedroom midnight blue with little twinkling stars, and a subsequent, more practical owner poured a steel-reinforced buttress (certain death) at the corner of the property in order to deflect drivers who did not make the curve on Brickell from coming into his living room. It was not an idle concern. That fortresslike construction is still there, now protecting the six-story office building that replaced the house. And no one has failed to navigate that corner since.

• • •

A friend from Virginia, who lived in the 1920s Old Spanish–style stucco house on Bayview Road in the Grove, whose ancestry included John Rolfe and Pocahontas, and whose manners, linens, and silver were gracious and aristocratic. She was a nice counterpoint to the free spirits in plentiful supply, like the girl whose pet dog was half wolf and the young man whose hot tub was on the roof of his house.

• • •

The remodeled coach house from the earliest days, across from Vanguard School, once the original location of Gulliver School before it moved to the ten-acre property it now occupies on Old Cutler. On festive Parents Days, when the noise level at Gulliver was at an all-time high on the outdoor playground, the agitated owner of the coach house always turned her stereo as loud as possible to drown out the speeches and children's voices. (I doubt it was noticed.)

• • •

The Old Spanish–style house farther down on Bayview, where you had to crawl through a double-hung window on the second floor to reach the sun roof, and the front door had no doorknob, just a hole. Nevertheless, when put up for sale in that condition, the asking price was more than $250,000.

• • •

Stroll along Main Highway and at the north corner of

Fuller, you will see the one-time home of the Coconut Grove Bank. A small, cream-colored building with barred windows and deco plaster trim, it was a mini version of what banks sought to look like years ago—substantial, decorated, fortresslike. When the bank built its new headquarters, on the corner of 27th Avenue and South Bayshore Drive (where it is today), its former premises were taken over by Dr. John C. Lilly in the interest of science, for a study exploring the language of dolphins and interspecies communication. It was a new and exciting idea—the thought that these animals might be understood and communicated with through a speech of their own. To this end, tanks of the creatures were introduced into the space, and dolphin noises were taped and decoded while pedestrians passing by on the sidewalk outside its tall double doors remained oblivious to the serious research on mammals being conducted inside the old bank building.

• • •

The beautiful, white two-story Colonial home of Charlie Crandon (the Miami city commissioner Crandon Park is named for) that once sat on ten green acres on Red Road like something out of *Gone with the Wind*. It's now the site of the Forest Development townhouses.

• • •

The happy sight of all the little girls from the Assumption Academy, standing on the corner of 15th Road and Brickell Avenue in their school uniforms, furiously waving tiny American flags one sunny morning as the motorcade of President Harry S. Truman sped past on his way to the dedication of Everglades National Park.

• • •

The day when raucous, shrill whistling drew us outside, where, in the leafy oak trees of our front lawn, a flock of more than a dozen mynah birds appeared, sharp-eyed and shiny black. They roosted high in the old branches, noisily talking things over, then, as a black cloud, moved on—a one-time event that even the Audubon Society could not fully account for, except to say they had had reports that some mynahs had been sighted in the vicinity.

● ● ●

The little dog from a neighbor's house in Coconut Grove that emerged each day at the sound of the squeaky stroller wheel and accompanied the baby and nurse on their daily walk to the bay like a self-appointed sentinel, turning back into his own yard on their return.

● ● ●

The puzzled homeowner whose house rested on that part of her lot that was in the Gables, but the backyard was in the city of Miami. When a burglary occurred one day, each police department insisted it was the other's problem. Since she paid taxes to both municipalities, it was frustrating, to say the least.

● ● ●

The elegant 1920s townhouse in the French Village in which the living room ceiling caved in as cocktail guests partied and the hostess carried a tot of Scotch in the head of her walking cane.

● ● ●

The house owned by a minister who kept wild baby quail in a glassed habitat outside his living room window and drove a little black MG with the license plate "REVS UP."

. . .

The small residential section hidden away in South Miami that has a railroad track running along all the backyards. The track sees only one train a day—promptly at five in the afternoon—a device to keep the railway's easement intact. One family living there dismissed what might be an inconvenience to some with the airy retort "Of course, we don't mind! It's how we know it's time for a drink!"

. . .

The sixty-year old "newsboy" who used to hawk his papers every day, rain or shine, at the corner of Flagler Street and NE 1st Avenue. The daily headline he shouted never varied. "Many dead! Many dead!" he promised. It sold lots of papers, and strangely enough there was almost always a story buried somewhere in the newsprint that lived up to his claim (the world being as it is).

. . .

Maynada—that street with a curious name, a father's tribute to his daughter, Mayna Adams.

. . .

The homeowner who enshrined his power mower atop a rock pile in his front drive, spray-painted it gold, and paved his whole front yard—a paean for those who love the verdant lawn but hate the means to that end.

. . .

The elderly little lady who lived in the small wooden house under the sausage tree on Cutler Road (where the

Snapper Creek subdivision now sits), who made wonderful white- and dark-chocolate coconut fudge and sea-grape jelly to sell to Sunday tourists.

• • •

The sight of the Duke and Duchess of Windsor in Burdines (formerly Burdine's) one afternoon, making some purchases before going on their way to the Bahamas, where HRH (His Royal Highness) served as governor. One onlooker marveled at how preserved and tiny they appeared. "Just like the little couple on top of a wedding cake!" she exclaimed admiringly.

• • •

The diffident switchboard receptionist at a downtown law firm who had to answer calls with the names of the attorneys: "Ruff and Reddy."

• • •

Soft, starry evenings. Bay breeze tinctured with salt air. An audience in front of the little white band shell in Bayfront Park. And in the spotlight, conducting the orchestra, a rotund, white-haired man in a white linen suit: Cesar La Monica.

• • •

Red Road and Blue Road—witnesses to the intersection of two colored pencils on the map of a surveyor.

• • •

Judge Ben Willard, a curmudgeon on the local bench whose hunting dogs kept his neighbors awake at night with their baying. Sleepless and annoyed, the neighbors felt they had no recourse to a fair day in court and so were happy when the judge finally moved out of town, taking his vocal hounds with him.

• • •

A single streetcar line used to run down the spine of the County Causeway alongside the deep-ship channel of Government Cut to the south. On hot summer days, a trip to the beach on the small trolley as it clacked and rocked its way across the tracks, its wooden windows open wide to the fresh salt breeze, was the best nickel ever spent.

• • •

Opening night for the new Lowe Museum in the 1950s: huge spotlights danced across the pristine white of the little building. Invited guests arrived in formal attire, marveling at the addition of a towering new fountain in the center of the circular drive, an unintended special effect, it was later revealed, caused by a large underground water main that had chosen that moment to burst.

• • •

The owner of a house on South Miami Avenue whose back garden eventually came under the scrutiny of the tall new condominiums rising on Brickell, thus depriving him of the privilege of privately relieving himself among his flowers.

• • •

The frustrated sailboat owner who tried to maneuver his craft under the old Brickell Bridge as a hurricane threatened. Since the mast was too high for clearance, he sounded his horn, notifying the bridge tender, who stopped the heavy downtown traffic and raised the span, only to have the wind gusts die and the sailboat sit becalmed just short of the opening. Several approaches, with the bridge opening and closing each time, were needed to coordinate the wind and the desired passage (accompanied by the cacophony from angry, homebound commuters blowing *their* horns). Syncopated choreography at work.

• • •

The old bachelor bookkeeper from Georgia who lived in a small flat above Captain Tom's Fish Market on the Miami River and whose hobby was repairing music boxes and pipe organs. He derived great pleasure from purchasing several sports jackets from a local thrift shop, which he saved for visits to relatives in the Georgia countryside. When a nephew would exclaim, "That's a good-looking sport coat, Uncle Robert," he always doffed it and said, "Here, it's yours."

• • •

Where the Omni Mall marks the Miami side of the Venetian Causeway, the Mayfair Theater once sat, a small perfect-as-a-pearl Art Deco movie house, where waiting patrons were offered hot or iced tea at saucer-size tables off the lobby. Next door, as traffic on the boulevard sped by, youngsters on sturdy Shetland ponies happily jounced around a sandy pony ring while admiring parents snapped dozens of blurry pictures for posterity.

• • •

Terminal Island (now called Fisher Island), off the County Causeway near Government Cut, once the preserve of William K. Vanderbilt, where the water was deep enough for his luxurious private yacht. His beautiful home survives as the clubhouse for a new development, and the charming, private villas that once housed his favored guests have become enviable, million-dollar acquisitions.

• • •

Like the hermit crab, who moves to a larger shell when he is no longer comfortable in his space, people move on too. Other shells, other houses, other places. But the echoes remain.

21

Outgoing **Tide**

Disappearing Acts

Has Miami been changed forever? Of course. That is what time is—change.

And there is no going back, except in memory. That is not to say change is bad or the past was perfect. It is simply to face an immutable fact—it is all *different*. And though we are allowed the backward glance, we are, after all, creatures of time and must continue toward the future, whatever comes.

If you are looking for observations from the 1960s to the present in this recollection, I am not going there, as the current phrase has it. For one thing, the changes in that time period were so rapid, numerous, and compressed, their exponential results are still being counted. This little book seeks only to conjure up a corner that was turned in the decades before the explosion of growth we see today eradicates the last of some remembered dwellings. Already, where older homes of no particular distinction sit, the lots are so valuable (pioneers, after all, *could* choose the best locations), those houses are being razed daily to accommodate huge new homes (huge because when you pay the steep and ever-escalating real estate taxes for that plot of ground, you want to build over most of it).

Furthermore, my intention has been to capture, if possible, a little of that gone-forever time when everyone who lived here could feel an integral part of the community. It was a time when you knew by name the salespeople who helped you, the butcher who supplied your cuts of meat, the car dealer, and your postman. You knew then who lived at most of the addresses in your neighborhood, and downtown held every resource needed. You knew with whom you were dealing because the Burdines owned Burdines; the Belchers, Belcher Oil; the Hectors, Hector Supply; the Pancoasts, the Pancoast Hotel, the Orrs, Orr Plumbing. The wave of ever-shifting corporate persona—here today but somebody else tomorrow—had not yet flooded the boardrooms.

In this inevitable process of change, more of the haunts of the early days should have been preserved. Miami is still being driven by its determination to embody the new, to shock and sizzle, and it daily destroys its past in the effort, rather than seeking to preserve or restore that which was the forerunner of what you see today. An irrevocable step. Many of the places *in situ* when this manuscript was begun have vanished or stand precariously in the path of some plan for future growth: Dr. Jackson's (Jackson Memorial Hospital) first office on SE 12th Street, the poinciana trees that line South Miami Avenue, and Brickell Park, to name a few. The days may be numbered for the Coconut Grove Playhouse and Parrot Jungle as well.

Happily, the constant in all of Miami's stories is its ability to attract a wide diversity of people of all tastes and backgrounds from all over the world. The reality is they are neither the first nor the last, but each brings a bit of influence that remains when it is time to move on. And in so doing, this unique city is created.

Time in its flight has left us a few reminders to prove that the past did indeed exist. The houses. The stories. The experience of it all. And if one listens carefully, the faint prophetic notes of "Farewell voices soft are saying . . ." on a lingering breeze.

Goodbye to all! Author at Brickell Avenue home in the 1940s.

I *ndex*

Note: Illustrations are indicated by boldface type.

If you enjoyed reading this book, here are some other books from Pineapple Press on related topics. For a complete catalog, write to Pineapple Press, P.O. Box 3889, Sarasota, FL 34230 or call 1-800-PINEAPL (746-3275). Or visit our website at www.pineapplepress.com.

The Everglades: River of Grass, 50th Anniversary Edition by Marjory Stoneman Douglas. This is the treasured classic of nature writing, first published 50 years ago, that captured attention all over the world and launched the fight to save the Everglades. The 50th Anniversary Edition includes an update on the events in the Glades in the last ten years. ISBN 1-56164-135-9 (hb)

Marjory Stoneman Douglas: Voice of the River by Marjory Stoneman Douglas with John Rothchild. Nationally known as the First Lady of Conservation and the woman who "saved" the Everglades, Marjory Stoneman Douglas (1890–1998) founded the Friends of the Everglades. This story of her influential life is told in a unique and spirited voice. ISBN 0-910923-33-7 (hb); ISBN 0-910923-94-9 (pb)

Florida's Past Volumes 1, 2, and 3 by Gene Burnett. Collected essays from Burnett's "Florida's Past" columns in *Florida Trend* magazine, plus some original writings not found elsewhere. Burnett's easygoing style and his sometimes surprising choice of topics make history good reading. **Volume 1** ISBN 1-56164-115-4 (pb); **Volume 2** ISBN 1-56164-139-1 (pb); **Volume 3** ISBN 1-56164-117-0 (pb)

Southeast Florida Pioneers by William McGoun. Meet the pioneers of the Palm Beach area, the Treasure Coast, and Lake Okeechobee in this collection of well-told, fact-filled stories from the 1690s to the 1990s. ISBN 1-56164-157-X (hb)

Florida Portrait by Jerrell Shofner. Packed with hundreds of photos, this word-and-picture album traces the history of Florida from the Paleo-Indians to the rampant growth of the late twentieth century. ISBN 1-56164-121-9 (pb)

The Florida Chronicles by Stuart B. McIver. A series offering true-life sagas of the notable and notorious characters throughout history who have given Florida its distinctive flavor. **Volume 1**: *Dreamers, Schemers and Scalawags* ISBN 1-56164-155-3 (pb); **Volume 2**: *Murder in the Tropics* ISBN 1-56164-079-4 (hb); **Volume 3**: *Touched by the Sun* ISBN 1-56164-206-1 (hb)

The Florida Keys by John Viele. The trials and successes of the Keys pioneers are brought to life in this series, which recounts tales of early pioneer life and life at sea. **Volume 1**: *A History of the Pioneers* ISBN 1-56164-101-4 (hb); **Volume 2**: *True Stories of the Perilous Straits* ISBN 1-56164-179-0 (hb); **Volume 3**: The Wreckers ISBN 1-56164-219-3 (hb)

Key Biscayne by Joan Gill Blank. This engaging history of the southernmost barrier island in the U.S. tells the stories of its owners and would-be owners. ISBN 1-56164-096-4 (hb); 1-56164-103-0 (pb)